G000167061

THAT'S THE TICKET FOR SOUP!

That's the Ticket for Soup!

Victorian views on vocabulary
as told in the pages of *Punch*

DAVID CRYSTAL

Bodleian Library
UNIVERSITY OF OXFORD

First published in 2020 by the Bodleian Library
Broad Street, Oxford OX1 3BG

www.bodleianshop.co.uk

ISBN 978 1 85124 552 9

Cover design by Dot Little at the Bodleian Library
Designed and typeset in 11 on 14 Bulmer by illuminati, Grosmont
Printed and bound in China by C&C Offset Printing Co. Ltd
on 120 gsm Baijin pure woodfree paper

British Library Catalogue in Publishing Data
A CIP record of this publication is available from the British Library

CONTENTS

INTRODUCTION
TO VICTORIAN VOCABULARY

There are times in the history of the English language when we see enormous spurts in the growth of vocabulary. The period after the Norman Conquest was one, when thousands of French words came into English. The Renaissance was another, introducing a diverse range of borrowings from dozens of foreign languages, as English ships explored the world. But the nineteenth century exceeded both of those, with a veritable explosion in the lexicon of science and technology as a consequence of the Industrial Revolution. From steam engines to motor cars, and textile mills to road building, the Victorian period might well be described as a brave new world of terminology.

Or a nightmare, according to some of the articles in *Punch* magazine. The concern is repeatedly addressed. How is it possible to avoid drowning in the flood of new jargon? Is it all necessary? And then, alongside the ever-increasing nomenclature of the sciences and factories, there was the even greater evolution of fashionable vocabulary and slang, the result of a class system whose divisions were becoming increasingly complex, as a new middle class elbowed its way in to sit, somewhat uncomfortably, between the traditional divide of upper and lower. A remarkable number of pieces in *Punch* during the Victorian era reflect the burgeoning and fast-moving slang of the elite, and how difficult it was for ordinary mortals to keep up with it. Not even personal names were exempt.

And then there was an additional complication: the new USA. When *Punch* began, in 1841, Anglo-American relations had improved dramatically since the Wars of Independence and of 1812, but ongoing disputes over trade, the boundary with Canada, and other issues provided a regular source of subject matter for articles and cartoons. And with America came Americanisms. Throughout the century, the distinctive vocabulary of the English emanating from the United States, and increasingly encountered in the British press, provoked continual irritation and mockery.

vii

Jargon, slang, Americanisms... When we look back at attitudes to vocabulary in the twentieth century, all three of these themes continue to loom large in books on style, usage manuals, and letters to the press or the BBC. And if Mr Punch was still around today, observing present-day trends, I don't think we would see much difference in *Punch*'s coverage from the topics illustrated in the following pages, which present the articles and cartoons that pilloried Victorian vocabulary between 1841 and 1903.

WHO WAS MR PUNCH?

If we look at the front covers of the magazine, we see him there, with the features of the puppet from the traditional Punch and Judy show, usually with a sardonic grin, and often accompanied by his dog Toby. His expression captures the satirical tone which was the magazine's hallmark. He would appear in its pages, sounding off about something that had caught his attention, always highly opinionated, and usually conservative in attitude. Novelty in language use always worries him, and he is very much a supporter of prescriptive linguistic attitudes, regularly deferring to such authorities from the previous century as Lindley Murray, John Walker and Samuel Johnson. He was of course a composite figure, his pieces being written by several journalists, but by associating his name with their articles he gave them an authoritative personal tone, and I have retained this fiction throughout the present book.

Punch was first published in 1841. Its subtitle, *The London Charivari*, was a reference to French satirical paper *Le Charivari*—the name alluding to a traditional form of popular justice in which someone was punished within their community by being dragged or mocked through the streets in a noisy parade. *Punch* would lampoon any and all British affectations—ostentatious dressing, the latest crazes, new inventions, sham gentility, developments abroad, the current political scene—and the affected or insincere use of language was a special target, along with the language that divided social classes. It drew attention to the abuses of the time, especially in its cartoons, with evident sympathy for the poor and unprivileged members of society. It prided itself on being a 'clean' journal—one that wives and daughters could read—unlike some of the other comic publications. And it changed the meaning of the word *cartoon* for ever, from a preliminary sketch for a work of art to a humorous and topical drawing.

Although *Punch* had a shaky start, with low and erratic circulation during its first year, it soon built up a following, and within a few years it was an English institution. A copy would be essential reading for most middle-class homes and would usually be found in such places as the waiting rooms of a doctor or dentist—which is where I first encountered it as a teenager. It ceased publication in 1992, though it had a few years of revival between 1996 and 2002. I find it an invaluable and unparalleled source of information about language use and attitudes of the times, and very much regret its passing.

THE VOICE OF AN AGE

I begin with the expression that has given me my title. It was the chief example in an article headed 'Elegant Phrases', published in the very first issue of the magazine in 1841 (p. 261). Mr Punch opens the piece with a paragraph that aptly sums up the aim of the present book.

> There are people now-a-days who peruse with pleasure the works of Homer, Juvenal, and other poets and satirists of the old school; and it is not unlikely that centuries hence persons will be found turning back to the pages of the writers of the present day (especially PUNCH), and we rather just imagine they will be not a little puzzled and flabbergasted to discover the meaning, or wit, of some of those elegant phrases and figures of speech so generally used by this enlightened and reformed age! The following brief elucidation of a few of these may serve for present ignoramuses, and also for future inquirers.

The irony, of course, lies in the fact that these weren't elegant expressions (for his predominantly middle-class readership) at all.

ELEGANT PHRASES

That's the Ticket for Soup.—Is one of the commonest, and originated several years ago, we have discovered, after much study and research, when a portion of the inhabitants of this wicked lower globe were suffering under a malady, called by learned and scientific men 'poverty,' and were supplied by the rich and benevolent with a mixture of hot water, turnips, and a spice of beef, under the name of soup. There are two kinds of tickets for soups in existence in London at present—

1. The Ticket for Turtle Soup, or a ticket to Lord Mayor's Feast. It is only necessary to add, these are in much request.

2. The Ticket for Mendicity Society Soup. Beggars and such-like members of society monopolize these tickets; and it has lately been discovered by a celebrated philanthropist that no respectable person was ever known to make use of one of them. This is a remarkable fact, and worthy the attention of the anti-monopolists. These tickets are bought and sold like merchandise, and the average value in the market is about one halfpenny.

How's your Mother.—This affectionate inquiry is generally coupled with

Has she Sold her Mangle.—'Mangling done here' is an announcement which meets the eye in several quarters of this metropolis; and when the last census was taken by the author of the 'Lights and Shadows of London Life,' the important discovery was made that this branch of business is commonly carried on by old ladies. The importance (especially to the landlord) of the answer to this query is at once perceivable.

How was *That's the ticket for soup* actually used? As it was a card given to beggars to go to a soup kitchen, it seems to have initially carried the meaning 'You've got what you came for, so now be off with you'. But it gradually softened, influenced by the wider use of *ticket* to mean 'the needed, correct or fashionable thing to do' (as in the expression, still heard, 'That's the ticket'). The dominant meanings became 'That's the way you'll get what you want' and 'That's the way you'll get rich.'

This is how Mr. Richard uses it, in Marcus Clarke's novel *For the Term of his Natural Life* (1874, Book 4, Chapter 5):

'I'm thinking of a trip to America,' said Mr. Richard, cracking an egg. 'I am sick of Europe. After all, what is the good of a man like me pretending to belong to 'an old family', with 'a seat' and all that humbug? Money is the thing now, my dear uncle. Hard cash! That's the ticket for soup, you may depend.'

The expression travelled widely outside Britain. We see it again in Peter B. Kyne's Australian-themed novel *Captain Scraggs* (1911, Chapter 18), when Scraggs boasts:

'I'll pull ten thousand out of this job.'
    Mr. Gibney whistled shrilly through his teeth.
    'That's the ticket for soup,' he said admiringly.

And it seems it is still travelling. A Google search brought to light the minutes of a district council meeting at a town in New Zealand which included extracts from a memoir of a road-building overseer. At one point we read:

Mr. Bell would tell me that he was off to Wanganui to get more money authorized for the bridges. With a broad smile, he would say, 'Have we started bridge so and so?'
    'Yes, Mr. Bell,' I would reply. 'It has been built and is being used, and so is another one.'
    'Good. That's the ticket for soup,' he would reply. This was one of his favourite sayings.

This was written in the mid-twentieth century, perhaps as late as the 1980s.

The eighteenth century had introduced the notion of 'politeness', and this became one of the foundations of nineteenth-century conversation. Elegance applied to everything, including terms of address and proper names. But there was a great deal of uncertainty about propriety, especially when a new relationship was being formed.

HOUSEHOLD WORDS

Young Person (*on taking a Situation with Maiden Lady*). 'In the Course of Conversation, shall I address you as *Miss* or *Mum*?'

Forty years later, the notion of elegance is still prominent, as seen in this item presented as part of a set of mock recommendations by a School Board (p. 55), but the writer adopts a more realistic tone:

> When you are introduced to a Duchess, and she asks after your health, it is hardly polite to say you are 'right as a trivet,' or 'A 1;' but it is quite possible for a popular member of the aristocracy to bring such expressions into use, in which case you would probably be right in using these peculiar idioms. A great deal will depend upon the time and nature of the introduction, the surrounding circumstances, &c. It is almost impossible to lay down any hard and fast rule which will be applicable at all seasons.
>
> *Vol. 80, 1881, p. 12*

Readers would certainly have recognized 'right as a trivet'—a fashionable idiom in the mid-nineteenth century, judging by the quotations in the *Oxford English Dictionary* (*trivet*, sense 4). It meant 'thoroughly right', the reference being to the way a trivet always stands firm on its three feet over a fire. The humour lies in the kind of person who would have used it—people like the poverty-stricken Peter Bunce in Thomas Hood's poem 'Dead Robbery' (1835) or the rowdy medical student Bob Sawyer in Charles Dickens's *Pickwick Papers* (1837, Chapter 50):

> 'Oh,' said Mr. Winkle the elder, looking rather grimly at Bob.
> 'I hope you are well, sir.' 'Right as a trivet, sir,' replied Bob Sawyer.

So, 'hardly polite' indeed, for most of the magazine's middle-class readers imagining a conversation with an aristocrat.

Mr Punch would regularly comment on the role of 'the surrounding circumstances' as the century progressed, but he could never have predicted the way notions of elegance would eventually extend to include Americanisms—even, it seems, associated with Duchesses (p. 47).

Without a 'hard and fast rule', there remained a hint of doubt over what was socially appropriate, even as late as the 1890s.

THE ETERNAL FITNESS OF THINGS

'And what is your Name?'

'Marian Watson. But my last mistress used to call me Mary, because Marian isn't a proper name for a Servant, she said.'

THE GENIUS OF SLANG

There's a jingle that captures the essence of slang:

> The chief use of slang
> Is to show that you're one of the gang.

'Gang' of course isn't restricted to youths and lawbreakers. It applies to any social group that uses vocabulary as a badge of identity. Doctors have their slang, as do lawyers, journalists and religious ministers. But the slang that was mainly the focus of Mr Punch's irritation—and he was always irritated by it, because he claimed he could not understand it—was the slang of the fashionable set. He commissions a long article on the subject, referring to writers known in Victorian times for their elegant style (Joseph Addison, Edward Gibbon, Lord Macaulay), great orators or elocutionists (Edmund Burke, Thomas Sheridan) and contemporary politicians (William Gladstone, John Bright). Probably least known to modern readers is Thomas Henry Buckle, whose *History of Civilization in England* was published in 1857.

> Slang is the fashion at the present moment, and it seems a fair prospect that the language in which ADDISON and GIBBON wrote, and in which LORD MACAULAY and MR. BUCKLE still continue to write, which was spoken by BURKE and SHERIDAN, and in which MR. GLADSTONE and MR. BRIGHT are still able to express their sentiments, will soon be overwhelmed by a torrent of extraneous expressions, coming we know not whence, and hurrying us we know not whither.
>
> Every day the Genius of Slang embraces a wider area beneath its extending wings. Its influence is no longer confined to the male youth of the nation, the class in whom we may expect to find the Athenian element developed, ever searching after novelty, or receiving it with open arms. Long since it penetrated into the Forum, and now we meet it in the Senate, and even the pulpit itself is no longer free from its intrusion.
>
> *Vol. 36, 1859, p. 231*

Genius isn't being used here in its modern sense of 'great intelligence'. It's more the personification of an immaterial notion, as seen in such phrases of the day as 'the genius of the age' or (with a negative connotation) 'the very genius of carnage and ill-luck' or 'the genius of disaster' (examples from the *Oxford English Dictionary* at *genius* 4, 6). An allusion to 'the genius of the language'—the particular properties thought to characterize the spirit of the English language—may well lie behind the writer's title.

What worries the writer most is the way it seems to be spreading throughout society—like a pernicious weed:

> When deformity is hidden, if only by a mask of words, a momentary advantage may be gained. But who can defend clothing beauty with the garb of ugliness? What can be said in favour of a dialect from whose repertory the beautiful woman, the eloquent statesman, the brave soldier, the stirring preacher, and the successful prize-fighter, may be all comprehended under the denomination 'stunner?'

THE PROGRESS OF SLANG

'Why, what a pretty new frock Alfred has!'
Prodigy (who picks up everything so readily). 'Ah, aint it a stunner!'

7

The article concludes:

> From wheresoever the Slang plant draws its sap,—from the East or from the West, or from suckers indigenous to the British soil,—it is a rank weed, and the sooner it is rooted up the better.

In other places, Mr Punch answers his own question. The slang weed is so deeply rooted because it is assimilated at a very early age.

Master Tom (who has been rebuked for making use of school slang). 'But Grandma', Slogging is derived from the Greek word slogo ($\sigma\lambda\acute{o}\gamma\omega$), to slaughter, baste, or wollop; and by compounding, you see—'

Grandma' is quite overcome by Tom's learning

8

In 'A chapter on slang', many more examples are given a poetic treatment. Some words are still used, or their meaning is clear from the way they are used in the verses. This glossary may be needed for those that are less familiar today, or no longer used.

baw—posh pronunciation of *bore*

beaver—a hat of various shapes; in the seventeenth century a tall top hat made of silk (imitating beaver fur)

bender—colloquial for a sixpenny coin (probably because it bent easily)

bob—a shilling coin (12 old pence)

bollinger—a narrow-brimmed hemispherical hat, topped with a button

brick—see p. 18

cheese/cheddar, the—the fashion, the best

cheese (verb)—discontinue (as today, *cheese it!*)

concern—property, estate, business (as today, *a thriving concern*)

crib—thieves' slang for a dwelling house, shop or pub

cut, go on the—get tipsy (perhaps from a short cut taken to a tavern)

cut, the—superior fellow (compare today, *a cut above*)

dem—posh pronunciation of *damned*

diggins—colloquial pronunciation of *diggings* 'lodgings' (compare *digs*)

fast—see pp. 18–19

fob—a small pocket in a waistcoat or waistband

gammon'd—deceived, especially by plausible talk

guv'nor—colloquial spelling of *governor*, with overtones of its other senses of 'guardian', 'ruler' or just plain 'mister' (see also p. 19)

mizzle—vanish, disappear (perhaps from Shelta *misli* 'go')

rigging—mocking, teasing (from *rig* 'trick, swindle')

rum—odd, strange (origin obscure, possibly from *Rom, romany* 'gipsy')

stashed—brought to an end (perhaps a blend of *stop* and *squash*)

stick—a dull or stubborn person (compare today, *old stick*)

ticker—any kind of watch

tile—a hat (from roof tile)

tin—money, especially silver coins (which, when worn smooth, resembled pieces of tin); Mr Punch has another view (see p. 18)

tizzy—a sixpenny coin (probably from *teston*, a sixteenth-century coin)

tog—see p. 23

turnip—an old-fashioned watch with a heavy silver covering

How debased in that tongue, once our glory and pride;
By a torrent of Slang how remorselessly dyed;
As this *Punch* has observed with a patriot's pang,
He devotes to his country this Chapter on Slang.

To its champions and friends, from the small to the big,
From my LORD BOBBY CAUDLE to little BILL PRIGG;
Punch addresses these lines, and he hopes they'll amend,
When he holds up to laughter 'our dashing young friend.'

Our dashing young friend of to-day never tells
The hotel he puts up at, or house where he dwells,
Of his Diggins perchance we'll hear something about,
Or his Crib, or Concern, Sir, or where he Hangs out.

Our friend has no pocket, he may have a Fob,
Though it holds not a shilling, it may hold a Bob;
It has not a sixpence, or any coin in,
Though it may have a Tizzy, a Bender, or Tin.

Our friend of to-day has no watch to his name,
'Tis a Ticker, or Turnip; if wrong, it goes Lame:
What the hour is he knows not, though able to say
How the Enemy goes, or what's His time of day.

Our friend knows of nothing that's strange, it is Rum;
His is not a companion, he's always a Chum;
Though his Chum is not staunch, yet he may be a Brick,
And though young men are fast, all things else so are Stick.

Our friend knows of nothing a plague, it's a Baw,
Though he drinks brandy Neat, he has ne'er had it raw;
His father's no father, but out of a joke,
He's the Guv'nor, Old Buffer, Old Cock, or Old Bloke.

Our friend of to-day has no coat, it's a Tog,
And he ne'er dresses well, though he Goes the whole hog,
He is then just the Cheddar, the Cut, Cheese, or Style,
Though his head bears a Bollinger, Beaver, or Tile.

Our friend prone to vices you never may see,
Though he goes on the Loose, or the Cut, or the Spree,
For brutally drunk, he's as Screwed as old Nick,
And you'll find him next morning, though Seedy not sick.

Our friend of to-day sees a Kid, not a child,
And he never gets steady, he Draws the thing mild;
A jest should be Knocked off, Cheesed, Shut up, or Stashed,
And a man's broken nose, is his Claret-jug squashed.

Our friend never suffers a fraud or a cheat,
He is Gammon'd, or Sold, or Let into it sweet;
He never retreats, though he Mizzles it quick,
Or he Slopes, Bolts, or Hooks it, or else Cuts his stick.

Our friend of to-day is not calm, he is Cool,
And a man who's not wise, must be Soft, or a Fool;
For a scolding, he always Comes in for a wigging,
A Rowing, a Jawing, a Lipping, or Rigging.

Mr. Punch thinks it high time his Shop to shut up,
He commends these remarks to each Darling young pup,
Who in slang words deals largely, and thinks it Dem rare,
Like our snobs, nobs, and footpads, to slang, and to swear.

Vol. 37, 1859, p. 22

Caudle and *Prigg* are fictitious surnames that *Punch* sometimes uses (as on p. 74). A *caudle* was a hot, thick, sweet drink, often given to new mothers and invalids. The name appealed to *Punch*, partly because it was associated with the aristocracy—after a royal birth, visitors to the palace (and members of the public) would be given 'the Queen's caudle'—and also because on special occasions (such as christenings) it was drunk out of little punch cups. *Prigg* (or *prig*) represented the opposite end of the social scale: it had a range of meanings, including 'thief, tinker, cheat, fool, fop'.

COLLOQUIAL EQUIVALENTS

Papa. 'Now my dear Girls, your Brother is receiving a most Expensive Education, and I think that while he is at Home for the Holidays you should Try to learn Something from him.'

Emily. 'So we do, 'Pa. We've learnt that a boy who Cries is a "Blub," that a Boy who Works Hard is a "Swot"—'

Flora. 'Yes, and that anybody you don't Like is a "Cad;" and we know the Meaning of "Grub," "Prog," and a "Wax!"'

On p. 6 we see Mr Punch referring to slang coming from 'the male youth of the nation', and it is the male pronoun only that appears in the poem. But women have their slang too, and this upsets him just as much.

FLOWERS OF MODERN SPEECH AND SENTIMENT

Our Gallant Colonel. 'And where and how have *you* spent the Summer, Miss Golightly?'

Miss Golightly. 'Oh I sat in a Punt with my favourite Man—a quite too *delicious* Man!'

He issues a severe warning, recalling *Impressions of Theophrastus Such*, by George Eliot, which had been published the year before. This was a collection of social commentaries written in the voice of a fictional male philosopher. One of the essays was headed 'Debasing the moral currency', by which s/he meant: 'lowering the value of every inspiring fact and tradition so that it will command less and less of the spiritual products.' The *Punch* writer must have read it, as one of Such's targets was 'a certain style of young lady, who checks our tender admiration with rouge and henna and all the blazonry of an extravagant expenditure, with slang and bold *brusquerie* [bluntness] intended to signify her emancipated view of things'. A *wrangler* was (and still is) a student taking the mathematical tripos at Cambridge University who gains a first-class degree; the name derives from the older sense of 'debater'.

DEBASING THE VERBAL CURRENCY
(A long way) after Theophrastus Such

'On 2nd inst., at the —— Street Police Office, a gentlemanly-looking young man, who refused his name, was fined ten shillings and costs for using bad language.'

MORAL.

Now, all you nice young Ladies,
Be warned by this, I pray;
Whoso murders the Queen's English,
For it will have to pay.

Respect the words your mothers
Have watered with their tears,
And against your slangy brothers
Shut tight your rosy ears.

Go and win Wranglers' places,
Go up in, and for, degrees;
But no more slangy phrases,
Dear young Ladies! if you please.

Vol. 77, 1880, p. 71

14

ENGLISH AS SHE IS SPOKE!!

Future Duke. 'What are you goin' to do this mornin', eh?'

Future Earl. 'Oh I dunno. Rot about, I s'pose, as usual.'

Future Duke. 'Oh, but I say, that's so rotten.'

Future Earl. 'Well, what else is there to do, you rotter?'

15

THE NEED FOR GUIDANCE

How should the flood of incomprehensible slang be handled? Mr Punch has a number of specific suggestions to offer. A phrase book? A dictionary? A catechism? Or all of these, for the fight needs every reinforcement it can get. In an early issue he provides an initial list of helpful definitions, choosing as his target the slang of 'fast men' (characterized in the explanation of *pump*). There are several contemporary references in 'The Fast Man's Phrase-Book' (p. 18).

Field Lane—A street noted for its poverty, squalour and crime. Charles Dickens describes it in *Oliver Twist*, for it is where Fagin has his hideaway: 'Near to the spot on which Snow Hill and Holborn meet, there opens, upon the right hand as you come out of the City, a narrow and dismal alley, leading to Saffron Hill. In its filthy shops are exposed for sale huge bunches of pocket-handkerchiefs of all sizes and patterns, for here reside the traders who purchase them from pickpockets.' Mr Punch is being naughty. It was not far from the Inns of Court, but lawyers would never have had chambers here.

Guffin—The name reflects a northern dialect word for a clumsy or stupid person. A Yorkshire dialect dictionary of 1862 defines a guffin as 'one who, from timidity, commits gross blunders, and is awkward in movement, with a spice of dulness to boot.' It became one of Mr Punch's favourite fictitious surnames (see p. 18).

Macauley—It's not possible to say exactly which Macauley is intended. There were various well-known singers, actors and comedians with this surname. It certainly isn't Lord Macaulay, whose spelling is different.

The Tipton Slasher—The nickname of William Perry, heavyweight prizefighter, born in Tipton, Staffordshire. He became all-England champion in 1850.

Paul Bedford—A popular English comedian, so well known that his way of talking was made the frontispiece of Albert Smith's *The Natural History of the Gent*, published in 1847. According to him, the 'gent' likes to imitate popular performers, and he quotes from Bedford, illustrating his distinctive pronunciation: 'Come along, my r-r-r-rummy cove; come along comealong-comealong! how are you? how d'ye do? here we are! I'm a looking at you like bricksywicksywicksies—I believe you my boy-y-y-y-y!'

Prince Albert—The husband of Queen Victoria, whom he married in 1840. Although he eventually became a highly respected figure, his popularity in Britain was still low at the time this article was written.

George IV—King from 1820 to 1830, remembered for his flamboyant costumes, and for his extravagant and profligate lifestyle. He had been described in 1814 by cartoonist George Cruikshank as 'The Grand Entertainment'. A *Times* obituary said 'There never was an individual less regretted by his fellow-creatures than this deceased king.' The reference to his 'blessed majesty' is a barbed joke.

Cremorne—Cremorne Gardens, a hugely popular leisure park in Chelsea, laid out in the grounds of Viscount Cremorne's London house. It opened in the 1840s with numerous attractions. The 'fast set' would have been there in force.

Artists have a phraseology of their own; actors indulge in technicalities only intelligible to themselves; lawyers and conveyancers practising in Field Lane, have a slang that is a dead language to others; and Fast Men likewise enjoy a verbiology that is only current amongst Fast Men, and never heard by any accident in respectable society.

A correspondent, who signs himself 'A converted Fast Man,' sends us the following specimens of the unknown tongue of the class which he has virtuously renounced:—

BRICK— A term of extreme laudation, applied, not to buildings, but to human beings. To be called 'a Brick,' is the highest compliment a Fast Man ever bestows. It means 'a capital fellow:' viz. 'GUFFIN is a Brick,' *i.e.* 'GUFFIN is every night at the Casino.' A 'regular Brick' is the superlative degree of 'Brick;' as, for instance, a Fast Man would call MACAULEY, perhaps, 'a Brick,' but the TIPTON SLASHER, in his estimation, would be (undoubtedly) a 'regular Brick.'

BRICKSY-WICKSY— For the meaning of this choice word, the reader is requested to ask MR. PAUL BEDFORD.

PUMP— A term of profound contempt. A Fast Man divides the human family into only two branches—the 'Pumps' and the 'Bricks.' These are the A'z and Z's of the living alphabet—all the rest are mere dead letters. Any one whose habits are opposed to those of a Fast Man, is necessarily a 'Pump.' If the person will not smoke, or sing, or drink, when asked, he is for ever stigmatised as a 'Pump.' If he will not make stupid speeches, or behave himself in a ridiculous, conspicuous manner, there is no hope for him—he is everlastingly condemned as a 'Pump.' We have no doubt that PRINCE ALBERT is frequently anathematised by the Fast Man as a Pump, because he does not contract debts, or build toy-palaces, or wear white kid inexpressibles, and commit similar breaches of good taste, which earned for his blessed majesty, GEORGE IV., the imperishable title of 'The greatest Gent in Europe.'

TIN—The Fast Man with any degree of self-respect never says 'money.' It is sometimes 'blunt,' occasionally 'rhino,' but most frequently 'tin.' 'Lots of tin' means a good sum of money. The origin of this word must have been taken from the cheeks of a theatre, which are expressive of so much money, and are made of tin. To hear two Fast Men talking about 'making much tin,' one would imagine they were in that particular trade, and had realised a good stock of the commodity; but it only relates to their financial affairs.

CLEANED OUT does not apply to the face, or person, or habitation, or mind of the Fast Man being in a clean state; but to his pocket having undergone that operation. It simply means that he has no more money, that is to say, 'tin.' 'Stumped out' has the same elegant import, 'stumpey' being another term for money.

MALT is a comprehensive term for beer. It includes ale, porter, stout, draught as well as bottled.

MALTY is indicative of the state of the Fast Man who is labouring under the effect of too much 'malt,' in the same way that BEERY is expressive of the mental condition of the Fast Man who has partaken of too much beer.

FRESH is not applied to the morning air, or new-laid eggs, or ancient venison, or news, or water just broke from the pump, or a lady's colour, but the state of the convivial Fast Man who has been drinking too liberally of spirituous liquors. Walk behind Fast Men or Boys at Cremorne, and the chances are, you will hear one of them say, in a tone rather proud than otherwise, 'Do you know, BILL, I was a little fresh last night.' It only means that he was a little 'elevated.' It is astonishing how rich the vocabulary of the Fast Man is in terms of intoxication. A regular ascending scale of drunkenness—a perfect ladder of inebriety—might be composed out of the abundant stock. It will only be necessary to specify a few. The nice gradations of meaning of these terms it would be almost impossible to explain to any but a Fast Man; and we are sure, consequently, our readers will not require the explanation. His drunken vocabulary comprises Lushy, Screwy, Groggy, Touched, Elevated, and innumerable others, which have been drawn by the Fast Man from a long course of experience.

GOVERNOR.— Father is a word always banished from the lips of the Fast Man. He never uses any other word but Governor. The wonder is, that he has invented as yet no corresponding term for Mother. The only one for it he ever delights in is the elegant phrase of 'Old Woman.'

Vol. 13, 1847, p. 213

Brick proved to be an endless source of fascination, and a couple of years later was given an article all to itself. Allusion is made to four personalities.

James Crichton (1560–1582)—A brilliant polymath, recalled in a historical novel of 1836 and referred to by many authors of the day, such as Thackeray and Dickens. The 'admirable' sobriquet is recorded from the seventeenth century.

Barnett Nathan (1793–1856)—Self-styled 'Baron', a well-known entertainer and dancing instructor, often mentioned in *Punch* articles.

Henry Brougham (1778–1868)—A leading figure in London society, designer of the brougham carriage, who became Lord Chancellor.

Buffoned—given its place in natural history. From the French naturalist Comte de Buffon (1707–1788), whose books on natural history continued to be influential into the nineteenth century.

DEFINITION OF A 'BRICK'

The meaning of this word, which has been lately introduced into our 'fast' Literature, has often puzzled us. If we judged of the structure of our present Society from the specimen of one of its 'Bricks', we should say it was of a very composite order, in which the Gent figured as the foundation and everything that was base. A 'regular brick' implies, we believe, the possession of all the Gentish, that is to say, vulgar accomplishments. Young men emulate one another in being Bricks. They smoke, dance, and sing, and run up bills,—and it is all done 'like Bricks.'

The attributes of a Brick, in fact, are universal. Like a pawnbroker, he takes in everything. He is versed in every possible and impossible grace and knowledge. Put down the Admirable CRICHTON, multiply by BARON NATHAN *plus* LORD BROUGHAM, and you have a perfect 'Brick'—a 'Brick' of the very finest clay, fit to adorn any palatial residence, or otherwise. We feel a library might be filled with the characteristics of the 'Brick.'

Until this extraordinary genus,—or, rather, if the reader will pardon the expression, genius, is thoroughly Buffoned, we are glad to clear away a little of the obscurity that at present reigns around the word by the following definition, which we take from the Indian letter of a Subaltern published in the *Times*. It is only such little straws, picked out one by one, that will ultimately show what the 'Brick' is really composed of:—

SHERE SINGH treats him *like 'a Brick.'* He has twenty men to guard him all day and night, and has a bottle of brandy placed on his breakfast-table every morning.

Ergo, to have twenty men continually hanging about your arm-chair, or round your pillow, and to have a bottle of Cognac every morning for breakfast, is to be treated 'like a Brick.' Gracious goodness! with temptations like these, who wouldn't be a 'Brick?'

Vol. 16, 1849, p. 152

REFINEMENTS OF MODERN SPEECH

Fair One (to devoted Swain, who has just put her Skates on). 'Ta! *Awf'lly* Ta!!'

By the nineteenth century, the original religious use of *catechism*—a question-and-answer guide to Christian religious teaching—had been extended to cover any book of instruction that used the same kind of dialogue. In the seventeenth century, such works were usually parodic in character, but by the nineteenth they had come to be genuine attempts at education. Oliver & Boyd were advertising an entire series of catechisms, including *Milligan's Catechism of English Grammar*, in 1842. They were very definitely serious works, with such titles as *A Catechism of Natural Philosophy*, … *Astronomy*, and … *Political Economy*.

Slang was hardly an appropriate subject, we might think, for such dignified treatment. Mr Punch thought otherwise. In distinguishing *nob* and *swell*, the Answerer (*A*) refers to the Marquess of Hastings. This was Henry Rawdon-Hastings (1842–1868), the fourth marquess, who held peerages in England, Scotland and Ireland, and who was known for his extravagant lifestyle. He died the same year that this article was written. Augustus Smith (1804–1872), evidently not in the same social league, was an MP and Lord Proprietor of the Isles of Scilly. The *four-in-hand* is a reference to the then fashionable method of doing up a necktie, the name probably deriving from the Four in Hand horse-driving club, founded in London in 1856. The swell's *tile* is his hat (see also p. 9), and if it is *out-and-out*, then it is fashionably perfect.

The article ends with a call for help to the lexicographer John Walker (1732–1807), whose works were still being referred to as authoritative in the Victorian era. He plays a major role in my book on Victorian pronunciation attitudes, *We Are Not Amused*.

A SLANG CATECHISM

Q. What is an Aristocrat?

A. A Swell, a Nob.

Q. Is there a distinction between a Swell and a Nob?

A. Rayther so. All Nobs are Swells, but a swell ain't necessarily a Nob.

Q. Give an example.

A. The MARKIS O' ASTINGS, he's a Nob and he's a Swell; MR. AUGUSTUS SMITH, in some Government hoffice or other, as goes about with Markisses and dresses no end—he's a Swell, but he ain't a Nob.

Q. Whence do you derive the appellation Nob?

A. From a door-handle. As there's always a'most a knob to a handle, so in society it's the handle to the name as makes the Nob.

Q. Into what classes do you divide Society?

22

A. Into Nobs, which includes regular Nobs: Swells, which includes Tip-toppers, Regular Swells, Cheap Swells, Gents, Snobs, and Cocky-waxes.

Q. What is a Regular Nob?

A. As aforesaid. Handle to name, tin, togs, and all complete.

Q. What is a Tip-top Swell?

A. Mostly Coves in four-in-'ands. From twenty to thirty-five.

Q. A Regular Swell?

A. He is a older cove—from thirty-five to fifty. He rayther runs to fat, but there ain't a speck on him anywhere, and his boots and tile are out-and-out.

Q. The terms Cheap Swell, Gent, and Snob require no explanation. What, then, is a Cockywax?

A. It's a term of endearment, and may include any of the above, or may be a class by itself, without a swell or nob in it. Cockywaxes are any age. If addressing a Cockywax you qualified it by prefixing 'old' or 'young.'

Q. You mentioned Togs, whence is this word derived?

A. Undoubtedly from the Latin *Toga*. 'Togs' means dress.

Q. When was the word *Cove* first used?

A. It was imported by the Romans, and was first used in an abbreviated form by the British whenever they saw a *Covinarius*, i.e., *a soldier in a war-chariot*.

Q. Explain and give derivations of the words *Trump*, *Brick*, *Chap*, *Guffin*, and *Bloke*. Also in each case give your reference.

A. I will. *Walker!*   [*Exit Answerer.*]

Vol. 55, 1868, p. 136

Mr Punch's etymologies are not always accurate. He gets *togs* right—there is a connection with *toga*—but he is guessing with *cove*. The etymology of this word isn't known, though it may have a connection with an old Scots word *coff* 'to buy', and thus meaning 'hawker', 'pedlar'. *Cockywax* is literally, *cock of wax*—*cock* in its sense of 'pre-eminent person', and *wax* alluding to a character as faultless as if the person was modelled in wax. An earlier expression (found in Shakespeare's *Romeo and Juliet*, was *man of wax*).

SPREADING EVERYWHERE

Slang wasn't restricted to the everyday speech of upper and lower classes. Several articles show how it was entering into the businesses and professions—to such a degree, according to this next article, that even Mr Punch feels he is out of his depth.

His reference to 'Brother Jonathan' is an allusion to Americanisms. Around the time of the Civil War, *Brother Jonathan* was the American equivalent of *John Bull*, eventually replaced by *Uncle Sam*. The reference to a manufacturer escaping to the 'Swan Stream' is obscure. Eric Partridge, in his *Dictionary of Slang*, thought this might be the Swan River in Perth, Australia, referring to the way the continent had become a popular destination for emigrants, especially after gold was discovered in the 1850s.

If Mr Punch found the jargon taxing, the modern reader will find it even more so, and a Glossary becomes essential.

benjamins—type of shaped overcoat
bob—shilling
broady—broadcloth
couter—sovereign
crib—dwelling, place
cut one's lucky—get away, escape
downey—soft as down
fakement—trimming, decoration
finnuff—five-pound note
gilt—money
kick [in the first circular]—trousers
kick [in the second]—sixpence
kicksies—trousers
mawleys—hands

Melton Mowbray—tightly woven woollen cloth from that town
moleskins—trousers (of moleskin)
monarch—one pound coin
mud-pipes—thick boots
peg—shilling
plush, pilot—types of fabric
quarter—five shillings
ready—spare cash
slap—fine quality
sov—sovereign
swag—plunder, booty
tick—credit
toggery—garments
trotter-cases—boots, shoes

THE SLANG OF THE SHOPS

Of a truth the English language is in a terribly sad way. What with the fever for French phrases that rages with some writers, and the rash of Greek and Latin that keeps breaking out in others, there will soon be very little of pure healthy English left; and of that little a portion will speedily be swamped in the flood of German compounds which is annually swelling here. ... Add to this the coarse vulgarities that Brother Jonathan has sent us, and the eruption of slang phrases wherewith we are infected, thanks mainly to the efforts of the authors of burlesques, and it will surely be acknowledged that the tongue of Mr. Bull is in a most unhealthy state.

Of all the evils that affect the health of his vocabulary, perhaps none are more injurious than the slang terms used in trade; for it is obvious that, as we are a nation of shopkeepers, words so used must soon be in everybody's mouth. Whatever phrase be coined for purposes of trade will speedily pass current in all commercial circles; and though it be as tasteless and uncouth as the bronze penny, few critics will care to raise their voice against it. Accustomed as we are to read of pig-iron being 'quiet,' and breadstuffs being 'dull,' of tallow being 'firm at rather stiffer rates,' or pork 'moving off slowly at previous quotations,' we are tempted by mere habit to incorporate these phrases among our purer English terms, and to use them in a while without a shudder at their vileness. Thus becomes our language more and more corrupted, and the work of purging it more loathsome and appalling. Even *Punch*, the modern Hercules, might shrink from the endeavour to cleanse the English tongue from the fouler than Augean filth which has been heaped on it.

As a sample of how slang is gradually supplanting the pure English of our Dictionaries, we submit to public notice a few extracts from a circular by a 'Cove,' as he would doubtless call himself, who shall be nameless, but who states that as a 'Slap-up Tog and Out-and-Out Kicksies Builder,' he is 'well known throughout the world by working-men':—

'Mr. Nameless nabs the chance of putting his customers awake, that he has just made his escape from India, not forgetting to clap his mawleys upon some of the right sort of stuff, when on his return home he was stunned to find one of the top Manufacturers of

25

Manchester had cut his lucky, and stepped off to the Swan Stream, leaving behind him a valuable stock of Moleskins, Cords, Velveteens, Box Cloths, Plushes, Doe Skins, Pilots, &c., and having some ready in his kick—grabbed the chance—stepped home with the swag—and is now safely landed at his crib. He can turn out Toggery very slap at the following low prices for Ready Gilt—Tick being No Go.'

What sort of 'working-men' are they to whom such slang as this is commonly intelligible, we think that any ragged schoolboy would be found able to guess. Men who work with 'jemmies,' as such slang-christened implements, one might expect to talk of 'mawleys,' and 'stepping homeward with the swag;' but that an English tradesman should apparently court custom from housebreakers and thieves by putting forth a circular in their peculiar phraseology, we own we should not have considered it in reason to suppose.

Here, however, is another sample of shop-slang, which tends strongly to confirm the guess for whom it is intended:—

'Upper Benjamins, built on a downey plan, a monarch to half-a-finnuff. Fishing or Shooting Togs, cut slap, 1 pound, one quarter and a peg. A Fancy Sleeve Blue Plush or Pilot ditto, made very saucy, a couter. Pair of Bath or Worsted Cords, built very serious, 9 bob and a kick. Pair of stout Broad Cords, built in the Melton Mowbray style, half a sov. Pair of Moleskins, built with a double fakement down the sides and artful buttons at bottom, half a monarch.

Mud pipes, knee caps, and trotter cases built very low.

N.B.— Gentlemen finding their own Broady can be accommodated.

The 'Artful Dodger' and his pals may find this comprehensible; but readers who have had a merely common education would be puzzled to translate it into ordinary English. Far be it from us to hint that Mr. NAMELESS chiefly deals with pickpockets and housebreakers, and therefore since his language to the customers he seeks; but really such a thought would fairly be excusable, for on no other grounds can we explain the fact of his writing in Thieves' Latin while his business is in London, and might surely be transacted in the language of the land.

Vol. 40, 1861, p. 54

Artful Dodger—Jack Dawkins, a character in Charles Dickens's *Oliver Twist*, the young leader of a gang of child pickpockets.

The allusion to Dickens is one of hundreds that populate the early issues of *Punch*. He was closely associated with it, because of his friendship with editor Mark Lemon, writer Douglas Jerrold and illustrator John Leech, though—as Richard D. Altick points out in chapter 2 of his authoritative account of its early years, *Punch: The Lively Youth of a British Institution 1841–1851*—Dickens never placed his own writing in it. The readers of the magazine would nonetheless have readily recognized in its captions and articles the kind of language used by the cockney population of the capital, having become familiar with it through Sam Weller in *The Pickwick Papers*, the criminal characters in *Oliver Twist* and many others. Dickens had a very keen ear for accent and dialect, and his novels are full of the pronunciations and colloquial expressions that formed the majority of Mr Punch's targets. The slang usages of the shopkeepers, servants and 'fast men' described above all have their antecedents in Dickens. (Their pronunciations are illustrated in the companion to this book, *We Are Not Amused*, such as the focus on cockney '*h*-dropping', and the substitutions of *v* and *w* that made Sam Weller one of the best-known characters of the 1840s.)

THE SLANG OF THE DAY
(*Fragment of Fashionable Conversation*)

Youth. 'A—awful Hot, ain't it?'

Maiden. 'Yes, awful!' (*Pause.*)

Youth. 'A—awful Jolly Floor for Dancing, ain't it?'

Maiden. 'Yes, awful!' (*Pause.*)

Youth. 'A—a—awful Jolly Sad about the poor Duchess, ain't it?'

Maiden. 'Yes—quite too Awful—' (*And so forth.*)

REFINEMENTS OF MODERN SPEECH

Female Exquisite. 'Quite a nice Ball at Mrs. Millefleurs', wasn't it?'
Male Ditto. '*Very* quite. Indeed, really *most* quite!'

The judiciary has to take its share of the blame, according to this next article. At the time, the main courts all met in Westminster Hall before their move to the Royal Courts of Justice in 1882. Lord Campbell was Chief Justice of the Queen's Bench. Henry Hawkins would later become a High Court judge. The *Regulae Generales* (General Rules) are the publications, written in a high style, which English courts promulgate from time to time for the regulation of their practice.

SLANG IN WESTMINSTER HALL

The other day LORD CAMPBELL, in his anxiety to save the time of the public, recommended Counsel to call a Brougham a 'Broom,' and MR. HAWKINS, with the same laudable view, suggested to LORD CAMPBELL to call Omnibuses 'Busses.' His Lordship immediately acted on the hint, and as there seems every disposition in the Court of Queen's Bench to carry out the novel idea of saving time by shortening words, we have much pleasure in referring the Bench and the Bar to the Flash Dictionary, from which many hints for curtailment may be adopted. Of course LORD CAMPBELL will never think of using the word gentleman in future, when 'Gent' will answer all the purpose, and 'Pal' will be an efficient substitute for learned brother. Perhaps a conference with the Lord Chief Baron—of the Coal Hole—might be the means of furnishing the Judges of the Queen's Bench with an appropriate vocabulary, which could be published under the head of *Regulae Generales*, and indictments might be shortened by allowing the use of the word 'fogle,' instead of pocket-handkerchief. If the idea is to be carried out, we would recommend the appointment of an officer, to be called the 'flash cove,' in place of the present Judges' Associate.

Vol. 30, 1856, p. 57

The Coal Hole was a popular tavern in the Strand, frequented by celebrities, and with a mock judicial theme, as seen in this advertisement from the *Era* theatrical newspaper. There is still a pub of the same name today, close to the original location.

COAL-HOLE TAVERN, FOUNTAIN-COURT, STRAND, Opposite Exeter Hall.—The LORD CHIEF BARON NICHOLSON has the honour to apprise his Friends that he has redecorated the Coffee-room of the above establishment, and that it will be ready for the reception of the Public on Monday evening. Chops, Steaks, Kidneys, &c., from the Patent Gridiron. Dinners, Soups, &c. Beds. 1s. 6d.

The JUDGE and JURY SOCIETY sits Every Night at Nine o'Clock. New Cases of thrilling interest.

MR. NICHOLSON respectfully intimates to those Friends whom business or pleasure may call to the neighbourhood of the Coal-Hole, that his exertions are now solely for his OWN BENEFIT.

The self-styled 'Baron' was the impresario Renton Nicholson (1809–1861). The 'new cases of thrilling interest' were generally *poses plastiques*—tableaux in which female models posed in imitation of well-known works of art, such as Cupid meeting Psyche.

A marriage in high life is called an alliance. People being generally prone to ape their superiors, this foolish word will soon come to be applied to marriages in middle life and low life. The necessary consequence will be, that a married couple will be called Allies. Already we speak of Captain So-and-So and his Lady instead of his Wife. It will next be Captain So-and-So and his Ally, and ultimately 'Me and my Ally' instead of 'My Wife and I,' or 'I and my Husband' will be a customary form of speech amongst the lower orders.

Vol. 43, 1862, p. 108

REFINEMENTS OF MODERN SPEECH

Fair Intense One. 'Have you seen the Old Masters at Burlington House?'

Bashful Youth (fresh from Marlborough, and better at Cricket and Football than æsthetic conversation). 'No—that is—I mean, Yes!'

Fair Intense One. 'Are they not really quite *too* Too!!'

THE AMERICAN INVASION

During the 1860s, Mr Punch and his associates became aware that there was a threat even greater than slang to what he called 'the pure well of English undefiled'—adapting an expression the sixteenth-century poet Edmund Spenser had used to talk about Chaucer. News from America regularly hit the British headlines, especially during the American Civil War, and along with the stories came new and evidently disturbing vocabulary, as seen in this article.

> The QUEEN's English is in great danger of being permanently debased by a vile word which has lately been introduced into it—the word 'Reliable.' This base word was first coined in America, and thence imported into this country. It is about the worst word, not immoral, in the English language. Yet it is coming into very general use; you can hardly open a newspaper wherein it does not occur; and that even in leading articles written by educated men who ought to know better than, at this crisis especially, to employees such an illiterate Yankeeism.
>
> As Rely is to Deny, so is Reliable to Deniable. Is it not? Deniable, that may be denied. Reliable, that may be relied. But to say that a report or an assertion may be relied, is to talk nonsense. Intelligence may be said to be capable of being relied on. But Reliable is not that may be relied on, any more than Deniable is that may be denied on.
>
> All manner of persons are hereby commanded, in the name of the QUEEN, to cease from debasing HER MAJESTY's English by using the spurious American solecism, Reliable; and, instead thereof, when they want an adjective to signify that this or that statement may be depended on, are advised to use the genuine English compound, Trustworthy.
>
> *Vol. 40, 1861, p. 237*

Mr Punch was wrong. *Reliable* in its 'trustworthy' sense—'a person or information that may be relied on'—is known from the sixteenth century. It was the sense as 'dependable', said of a product or service being 'consistently good in quality', that emerged from America at the end of the eighteenth century. Its role in the language of science (*reliable results, reliable measurements…*) made its use unexceptionable by the end of the century.

But *reliable* continued to irritate him for over a decade. In a similarly named article, he takes another shot at it. Then, as is usually the case with neologisms that cause initial upset, familiarity breeds content. Other new words thought to be Americanisms take its place, and gradually the one that once caused such anxiety becomes unremarkable. Nobody today would think of *reliable* or *enjoyable* as American, and indeed it is unlikely that the USA had any role in the development of the sense from 'capable of being enjoyed' to 'actually being enjoyed', 'affording pleasure', for its first recorded use in the *Oxford English Dictionary* is by Alexander Pope in 1743:

> The Evening of our days is generally the calmest, & the most enjoyable, of them.

Another citation is from one of Charles Dickens's letters during the very decade when Mr Punch was complaining, in 1867:

> This passage in winter cannot be said to be an enjoyable excursion.

The use in Britain of *Americanism* to condemn any new word is something that is still found today.

An interesting point is the comment that 'the word is not in Johnson'. The reference is to Samuel Johnson's *Dictionary of the English Language*, first published in 1755. It was still considered the primary authority for the use of words over a century later, and would continue to be so until superseded by the project initiated by the Philological Society, *A New English Dictionary on Historical Principles*, that began publication in 1884. This would later become the *Oxford English Dictionary*. Mr Punch's deference to Johnson as an arbiter of lexical usage can be seen again on pp. 37 & 41.

AN IMPROPER EXPRESSION

'The most enjoyable number was the symphony,' writes a musical critic
in a notice of a Concert. This word 'enjoyable' is one of those novel
expressions that have of late been intruded into the English of the Press
and the Platform. Enjoyable, that which may be enjoyed; analogy defines
it, for the word is not in Johnson. In the foregoing connection it means
most productive of enjoyment. The symphony, described as having
been enjoyable when it was played, would have been equally enjoyable
if it had been murdered, or never been played at all. It would have been
enjoyable—that is, capable of being enjoyed —whether it was actually
enjoyed or not. To say that a composition, performed at a Concert, was
enjoyable, is either to represent that it was capable of being enjoyed by
a lover of music, or else to suggest that it might have been enjoyed if it
had been properly performed, or could have been heard. A dinner is
eatable, and likewise enjoyable, but in being eaten it, if enjoyed, is more
than enjoyable. This word 'enjoyable' sounds like an importation from
the United States. Though not so base a coin as 'reliable,' it is still not
sterling, and has the ring of a dollar.

Vol. 64, 1873, p. 168

'The Press and the Platform' was a frequent expression of the age.
Newspaper editor W.T. Stead, in an article headed 'Government by
journalism' in *The Contemporary Review* (May 1886), sums it up:

> the absolutism of the elected assembly is controlled and governed
> by the direct voice of the electors themselves. The Press and the
> Platform, of course, do not mean the printed words of a news-sheet or
> the wooden planks of a platform. They are merely expressions used
> to indicate the organs by which the people give utterance to their will,
> and the growth of their power is indicative of the extent to which the
> nation is taking into its own hands the direct management and control
> of its own affairs.

Mr Punch can't resist another dig at *reliable*, but his focus on *velocipede* as an Americanism is right this time. The use of this noun as a verb was rare—indeed, it is still (in 2020) not recorded in the *Oxford English Dictionary*—but it gives him the chance to make a political point.

The 'Alabama difficulty' is a reference to an incident in the American Civil War when the South bought warships built in British shipyards, disguised as merchant vessels to hide from British neutrality laws. The *Alabama* was launched in 1862, and destroyed many Northern ships before angry protests from the US government stopped the trade. A demand for huge compensation from Britain was at the heart of the 'difficulty' alluded to. The matter wasn't resolved until the Treaty of Washington in 1871.

WELCOME VERBAL STRANGER

Our well of English, once pure and undefiled, has derived a fresh increment from America. By intelligence from Yankeedoodledum we are apprised that:—

> 'At Cleveland, on Saturday, May 15th, FERD. HAWLEY, of Rochester, N.Y., velocipeded fifty miles in three hours forty-one and a half minutes.'

Welcome new verb 'to velocipede;' welcome equally with 'reliable.' British journalists will do well to take up this latest Americanism instantly, and make frequent use of it. Very possibly the abuse of England which the Yankee papers teem with, is in a very great measure occasioned by the contemptuous avoidance of their phraseological novelties which the higher part of our Press persists in. If the leading literary organs of this country will only follow the example of their inferiors in adopting every American addition to the English language as soon as it comes over, and employing it on every possible occasion, they will perhaps do far more than they could by any argument towards a settlement of the *Alabama* 'difficulty,' and the establishment of cordial relations with the United States.

Vol. 56, 1869, p. 266

The *Alabama* affair was still big news the following year:

AMERICAN SLANG GRAFFITI

People who have any reverence for 'the pure well of English undefiled,' must wish that the Americans would let that well alone, and not defile it with such hideous corruptions as the following:—

> 'One of the papers lately, instead of recording that the President had gone on an excursion, simply announced that he had 'excurted.' The other day we read that 'Erie' was injuncted. A paragraph in an evening paper was headed thus—'A woman Burgled Nine Times in Ten Years.'

Fancy the dismay of dear old DR. JOHNSON at reading such uncouth phraseology as this! Imagine him devouring Yankee newspapers for breakfast! With how many a cup of tea could he gulp down, without choking, their grammarless contents! And when afterwards discussing them in critical cold blood, with what rotundity of phrase would he give vent to his just wrath. Conceive the Great Lexicographer admitting to his Dictionary such excrescencies as: 'Burgle, verb active, To break into a dwelling-house,' or, 'Excurt, verb neuter, To go upon a journey.' What groans, and grants, and snorts of furious indignation he would forcibly emit on meeting with a sample of New English such as this:

> 'We have interviewed the cuss who quilled our yester's Editorial, and in this connection we may bigtype our assurance that the news which had been wired to us was regular reliable, as our reporters are injuncted from letting slide our reputation by telegramming fibs.'

Assuredly, if speech be silver, men who coin such phrases, which indeed should never become current, ought to be indicted for uttering false money. As a set-off to their claim for *Alabama* compensation, our Yankee friends should pay us for the injuries inflicted on the English language by word-inventing writers for the Trans-Atlantic Press.

Vol. 58, 1870, p. 44

ANOTHER PRETTY LITTLE AMERICANISM

Englishman (*to Fair New-Yorker*). 'May I have the Pleasure of Dancing with you?'

Darling. 'I guess you may—for I calc'late that if I sit much longer here, I shall be taking Root!'

Mr Punch was right when he picked on 'snappy' as a popular American-ism. The *Oxford English Dictionary* (*OED*) distinguishes three senses emerging in the last decades of the nineteenth century:

— 'Cleverly smart, bright, or pointed (of language, etc.); full of "go"; brisk.' First recorded in 1871 as used by Mark Twain.
— Neat and elegant; smart, 'natty': *snappy dresser*, someone who dresses in a stylish or natty manner. First recorded in 1881, the *OED* actually citing this article.
— 'Having a brisk smack or flavour.' First recorded in 1892.

He found it all very confusing.

THE NEW WORD

Punch. What do you think of this glass of Curaçoa and brandy?

Gilded Youth. It is very snappy.

Punch. That's a nice-looking girl over the way.

Gilded Youth. She is very snappy.

Punch. You had a thousand to twenty about *Peter* for the Hunt Cup at Ascot, hadn't you?

Gilded Youth. I had. It was a very snappy bet.

Punch. May I ask you what is the meaning of the word 'snappy'?

Gilded Youth. It is the English for cheek.

Punch. Cheek?

Gilded Youth. Yes, the French word 'cheek.'

Punch. Ah, *chic*! 'Snappy' is an American word, I believe. You have been in America?

Gilded Youth. No; but the Editor of the *Sporting Times* has, or ought to have been, as he introduced the word into England.

Punch. And what's the etymology?

Gilded Youth (*puzzled*). Eh? Ettie, Molly—who? Don't know her. Is she snappy? Have a drink, old chappie, and—(*sings*)—'Let us be Snappy together!'

Vol. 80, 1881, p. 310

Along with *reliable*, the verb *claim* was a regular target of Mr Punch's criticism in the early 1860s.

MORE YANKEE SLANG

One serious evil resulting from the abominable Civil War still raging in America, is its tendency to corrupt the English language. Despatches written by Northern generals are published in English newspapers, and almost all of them contain disgusting Yankeeisms, which are copied by many British journalists who ought to know better. Some new solecism is continually turning up in these illiterate compositions, and, being adopted and repeated in other writings of the same description, soon becomes current Yankee coin, as base as shinplasters or cardboard-stamps, which must not be suffered to pass in this country with sterling English. Some of these counterfeits have been already nailed to our counter, and we must now affix one more.

The last new mintage of American vocabulary smashers is the verb 'To claim,' used as signifying to allege, assert, or maintain. Such and such an officer, for instance, is said to claim that he has taken so many guns and prisoners. To pretend that he has taken them is what might naturally be supposed to be meant; because 'to claim' is to 'demand of right,' to 'require authoritatively;' and when it is said that a man claims to have done something, and especially something that is improbable, what seems to be implied is that he demands credit for his statement to that effect, which is doubted.

In the sort of Prospectus of a 'General Basis of the Society of the Lyceum Church of Spiritualists, Boston, U.S.A.,' occurs the following sentence:—

'The members of this Society claim that the soul of man is immortal.'

The ludicrous misuse of the word 'claim,' above instanced, may serve as an example, which gregarious, imitative, and unthinking writers, who are too apt to contract vulgar and villanous idioms, are hereby implored to avoid.

Vol. 43, 1862, p. 65

Two years later, he is still angry about *claim*.

AVOID AMERICANISMS

Solicitude for the English language compels us to quote the following telegraphic message from New York:—

> 'Fourteen of the Vermont raiders have been captured and imprisoned at St John's, Canada East. Two of them claim to hold officers' commissions in the Confederate service.'

'To claim,' according to DR. JOHNSON, is 'to demand of right, to require authoritatively.' In the statement above cited, it is alleged that two 'raiders,' who had fallen into the hands of the Federals, claim to hold commissions in the service of the Federals' enemies. As if we were meant to understand that it was in the power of their captors not only to prevent them from serving as officers on the other side, but also to grant or refuse them commissions to serve on that side, and fight those who had captured them.

We beg that, whenever any of our readers, and especially our brethren of the minor Press, have occasion to say that a person pretends or professes to be or to do this, that, or the other, they will say that he pretends or professes, and not that he claims, to be or do it. What is our objection to the word 'claim' in the sense of 'pretend?' ... Because 'claim' in the sense in which it is, as above, employed by Americans, is a euphemism for words which plainly impute deception, and its customary use implies the habitual extenuation of fraudulence prevalent amongst the people who are accustomed to use it. If ever we get generally to say claim instead of pretend, there will be good reason to doubt that we are as honest and truthful a nation as we claim to be considered.

Vol. 47, 1864, p. 207

The irony, of course, is that the word in this sense ('assert a claim to be'—not 'pretend', as he asserts) has a history that antedated America. The *Oxford English Dictionary* has a record of it from the fourteenth century. It seems to have died out at the end of the sixteenth, before being renewed in the sense of 'contend, maintain, assert' in the USA some 250 years later. A church tract in 1565 has a strikingly parallel usage: 'He that may call himself Lord and God may easily claim himself to be more than a man.'

41

In this next article, *reliable* turns up yet again, and, as with his previous comments (p. 33), Mr Punch is unaware that *obliviate* had a history of usage in Britain dating from the late seventeenth century—a first recorded usage in 1661, according to the *Oxford English Dictionary*. What he is objecting to with *recuperate* is not the word itself, which as a transitive verb has a history in English dating from the sixteenth century ('recuperatyng your helth', 1542), but the intransitive use ('to recover from illness'), which is first recorded in an American magazine in 1843.

The *Etna* in the opening sentence refers to the the SS *Etna*, travelling for the Inman Line between Liverpool and New York. General Ulysses S. Grant was the leader of the Union Army in the Civil War. John Baldwin Buckstone (1802–1879) was an English actor-manager and playwright.

PRESIDENT'S ENGLISH

Another Yankeeism nearly as illiterate as 'reliable' has just been imported by the *Etna* from New York, in one of REUTER's telegrams. This communication, one of those evil ones which corrupt good language, informs us that GENERAL GRANT is very ill, and that, 'as the army is about to settle into winter quarters, it is urged by GENERAL GRANT's physicians that he should go home to recuperate.' Some years ago MR. BUCKSTONE, in a farce, acted a Yankee's part, in which he had to say, 'If I live from July till eternity, I never shall obliviate this here go.' The formation of 'recuperate' from *recupero* may be more defensible than that of 'obliviate' from *obliviscor*, but still 'recuperate' is a needless corruption of Latin. Why not stick to 'recover?' Besides the French word *récupérer* has a distinct meaning, and signifies to retrieve. An American might, without any impropriety beyond that of affectation, talk about taking action to recuperate his dollars, but how can people who call themselves members of the Anglo-Saxon family, use such language? As for you who owe allegiance to HER MAJESTY, and are in duty bound to maintain the purity of the QUEEN's English; consider all such English as 'Recuperate' President's English, spurious, base, villanous; pray you, avoid it.

Vol. 46, 1864, p. 19

The best examples of Americanisms are those where, as Mr Punch says in this next article, a new word relates to a new thing. But when he says 'turning, as their manner is, a substantive into a verb', he is wildly off target, for this practice had been a routine function of English grammar since the Middle Ages. It is one of Shakespeare's favourite word-creating practices, seen in dozens of places—*he pageants us, I eared her language, he childed as I fathered...* There's a very full list under the theme 'Functional Shift' in the book *Shakespeare's Words* (*see* Further Reading, p. 99).

WE WILL TORPEDO THEM

'As yet,' says a contemporary, in an article urging the importance of the torpedo as a weapon of offence and defence in naval warfare, 'the science of torpedoing has never been thoroughly investigated in this country.' Here we have another new word, and, what is more, another new thing, come, as usual, from America. To employ torpedoes effectually against ships was an American achievement, and to call their employment 'torpedoing' is American speech. Turning, as their manner is, a substantive into a verb, the Americans have made one more addition to their mother tongue for us. Henceforth torpedo is to be conjugated in English grammars—'I torpedo, thou torpedoest, he she or it torpedoes,' and so on through all moods and tenses, the most important of which, in regard to making all due provision to act it out in case of need, is the Indicative Mood, Future Tense, First Person Plural—'We shall torpedo,' in the event of having our coasts invaded. Mind that.

Vol. 62, 1872, p. 222

As a grammatical footnote, the article also illustrates how writers of the age were following the prescriptive rule, emphasized since the eighteenth century, that insisted on a distinction between the auxiliary verb *will* (as used in the title, to express a definite intention) and *shall* (as used at the end of the piece, to express solely future time).

During the middle decades of the century, Mr Punch saw Americanisms everywhere. In this next article, *secesh* is clearly one, but he is wrong about *quite*. The usage *quite + a + noun* had long been used in Britain: we find *quite a scandal* in Pope, *quite a humourist* in Jane Austen. He also needs some grammatical help, for *quite* is an adverbial intensifier, not an adjective.

MORE AMERICAN SLANG

Her Majesty's subjects are hereby cautioned against the use of certain American corruptions of the QUEEN's English, besides those which we have already warned them to avoid, newly imported into this realm. The words of which we now deprecate the employment, have appeared in divers Yankee newspapers, and in sundry accounts, by officers in the Federal army, of their own exploits, written in a style which closely resembles that wherein clever thieves are accustomed to relate their adventures. One of these vile expressions is the spurious noun-substantive 'Secesh,' or 'Secesher,' meaning a person who has seceded from the American Union, and, who, in correct and established English, would be called a Seceder. The other is the genuine adverb 'quite,' ridiculously used as an adjective; as 'quite a number,' meaning a large number. It is hoped that this notice will render all loyal Englishmen careful to eschew these two abominable Americanisms.

Vol. 42, 1862, p. 133

The expression 'The Queen's English'—first used with reference to Elizabeth I—had become very popular by the 1860s, as illustrated by the best-selling book published by the Dean of Canterbury, Henry Alford, in 1864: *A Plea for the Queen's English.*

There is a genuine American creation in an article written a few years later. The allusion is to the way, since the end of the eighteenth century, American politicians had used the stump of a large tree as a platform for a speech. George Washington was one of the first. *On the stump* then developed to mean 'go about making political speeches'.

This issue of *Punch* came out during the year of a general election, in which William Gladstone and John Bright had prominent campaigning roles. Gladstone's Liberal Party defeated the Conservatives, and he became prime minister. Bright was reputed to be one of the best orators of the age.

AMERICANISING OUR LANGUAGE

If our forefathers get the papers in the Elysian Fields, they must be greatly puzzled by some of the expressions the writers now use. For example, when they read of 'the bad effects of the stump upon our most eminent men,' the meaning they are likely to extract from such a passage is, that our most eminent men are beside themselves with toothache, a painful impression which they probably exchange for the very bewildering notion that this Stump is some new musical instrument, with which our leading statesmen amuse themselves in their leisure hours, and perhaps delight their Constituents, when they read farther on of 'Mr. Gladstone's and Mr. Bright's performances on the stump.'

Vol. 55, 1868, p. 194

The word never really caught on in Britain. The *Oxford English Dictionary* adds a note on the British usage: 'though now common, it is still felt to be somewhat undignified.' And, certainly, those who used it in the Victorian era seem to have done so rather apologetically. Mr. Bright, in an 1879 address, still felt the need to explain its origin: 'We have seen the archbishops and bishops ... doing what is described in America when they say a man has taken to the "stump".'

Just occasionally and rather reluctantly, Mr Punch seems to have something positive to say about a new usage—but only because it is not as bad as it might have been.

AMERICAN ENGLISH

The Yankees are said to have lately coined another new word to express the act, sometimes committed even in the United States, of a man who kills his wife. They call it 'uxoricide.' This is better than most of their additions to the Dictionary. They might have denominated wife-slaughter conjugicide; which would have been ambiguous. 'Uxoricide,' having been established as a current expression, must of course be well balanced with a name to signal the converse deed, which, by parity of nomenclature, will be termed mariticide.

Vol. 66, 1874, p. 29

Whether it is American or not is actually debatable. The first recorded use of the word meaning 'act of wife murder' is in the very British *Fraser's Magazine for Town and Country*, published in London. In an 1854 issue we read of an English clergyman who complains:

I cannot peruse an English newspaper for ever so short a period without witnessing such a detail of premeditated murders, suicides, infanticides, matricides, patricides, uxoricides, and fratricides, as never disgraced any other nation on the earth, however barbarous or uncivilized.

In the sense of 'wife-murderer', the first recorded use is indeed in an American source—the 1860 edition of Worcester's *Dictionary*—but London's *Fortnightly Review* seems to be using it routinely in 1887:

Adultery, incest, uxoricide, usually by poison, prostitution, are terribly frequent.

A more positive attitude towards Americanisms grew noticeably during the 1880s. It followed the marked improvement in diplomatic, military, and economic relations between Britain and the USA which led to what American historian Bradford Perkins refers to as the 'Great Rapprochement' between the two countries—the first signs of the 'special relationship' so often mentioned today—and dates it from 1895. American pronunciation and vocabulary became more favourably regarded, and indeed became quite fashionable—so much so that foreign visitors to Britain were sometimes left confused. *Punch*, as usual, was ahead of the game, with this 1888 cartoon.

A SOCIAL DIAGNOSIS

Fair Visitor. 'There's that lovely Woman again. I wonder who she is?'

M. le Baron (an experienced observer). 'Madam, I tink she must be an *English Duchess*, because she is ver pretty, she dress vell, she speak sroo her Nose, she say, "You *bet*," and she talk about *Dollars* and *Cars*!'

WORRYING TIMES

Americanisms were not the only target of Mr Punch's scorn. Any word that was, in his opinion, overused, inappropriate, pretentious or likely to give offence would sooner or later receive a telling off—if not from him, then from a correspondent. This one signs himself *Pertaesus*—Latin for 'wearied, bored, disgusted'.

A WORD AND A WORRY

In the language of journals and reviews, *Mr. Punch*, there are certain—and uncertain—words and phrases, which, like some dramatic productions, get repeated with such frequency that they may be said to have a 'run.' In addition to 'elastic,' 'elasticity,' 'tension,' 'strained relations,' and so forth, an old word has lately been adopted, seemingly in a new sense, to express a particular shade of meaning—the word 'fairly;' as 'fairly proficient,' 'fairly industrious, 'fairly successful.' It appears intended to signify something more than 'moderately' or 'passably,' and something less than 'fully' or 'perfectly,' perhaps as nearly as possible 'satisfactory in the circumstances, all things considered.' But now it has come to recur so very often, that its repetition is felt to be considerably tiresome, like the posters on the railways, at station after station, advertising soap, and cocoa, and mustard, and corn-flour, which in interminable succession weary the passenger's mind and eye. 'Fairly,' indeed, may be a fairly handy term; but isn't it rather unfairly hackneyed, and all the rather that it is so vague as to be scarcely quite intelligible, whilst it constitutes a tautology which ought to be looked to, inasmuch as it decidedly amounts to a bit of a bore. In a fairly critical spirit, I trust, of comment on a trivial and slightly tiresome expression, permit me to express myself

    Yours particularly

    Pertaesus

Vol. 87, 1884, p. 270

NOTA BENE

Little Girl (*at South Kensington*). 'Oh, do Look, Miss Skimble! There's a Funny Thing!!'

Governess. 'My dear, how often have I Told you not to Use that Word *here*. Government object to it. You should Say "Curious" or "Remarkable." Recollect that!!'

Pertaesus mentions *elasticity* in his list of overused words. Mr Punch had already found it among the clergy.

EPISCOPAL ENGLISH

How much it is to be wished that they who have taken in hand to revise the Authorised Version will so mend as not to botch and cobble it. Pity it will be if that pure well of English undefiled have its chaste waters polluted with slipslop such as that wherein, mostly, our modern Prelates are wont to compose occasional prayers. In an epistle lately addressed by three right reverend Bishops to the London Clergy, recommending certain special missions within their several parishes for the conversion of the ungodly, you will find these words:—

> 'We do not think it necessary to lay down special rules for the conduct of the mission. There must be much elasticity in such an attempt to make it suit the different characters and needs of various parishes.'

Now, Sirs, this word 'elasticity,' in the sense of suitableness, is novel. No doubt it was engendered of the very greatly increased abundance of India-rubber which has come, within these last few years, into use. It is a word much affected by Ministers and Parliament-men, and also by political leading-article writers. In the Vestry it were a word especially in place, but as particularly out of place in the pulpit. It is altogether a secular, mechanical, and material-scientific word, fit only to be employed in regard to the management of material and worldly affairs. No poet would use it in serious verse; neither should a Clergyman in a sermon, charge, pastoral, or any other communication touching spiritual things, the rather that it has a significance more or less suggestive of humbug. An upstart expression foisted into the Text would be like a patch of new cloth, and that shoddy, sewn into an old garment of honest English make. That web is of a woof too precious to be pieced in with stuff of no more worth than a penny-a-line.

Vol. 64, 1873, p. 233

We need to appreciate the force of the last sentence. The reference is to writers who were paid at the rate of a penny a line, thus suggesting that the writing is routine, superficial and verbose.

Mr Punch's acerbic eye fell on everyone. Nobody was exempt. In this piece, he pillories the theatrical profession for its use of intensifying words. The Rubini referred to was Giovanni Battista Rubini (1794–1854), described as the 'king of tenors', who toured widely in Europe between the 1820s and 1840s, performing in London each spring.

DRAMATIC DEGREES OF COMPARISON

Actors and managers are in the habit of playing sad havoc with the Queen's English in general, and the degrees of comparison in particular. We find from long experience, that a '*positively* last appearance' is *comparatively* the commencement of an arrangement of some duration, and that the more '*positively last*' anything theatrical may be, the more superlatively remote it is in all probability. RUBINI had six 'positively last engagements' and nearly as many 'final retirements' from the stage, which were of a nature to put an end to all our preconceived notions of finality. The Adelphi Company has lately been outraging the degrees of comparison at the Haymarket, by showing that positively six may mean comparatively twenty-four, or thirty, as success may warrant. We congratulate the manager on his audiences having become 'large by degrees, and beautifully more,' a result that may readily excuse his having taken a perverted view of the degrees of comparison, in the announcements put forward in his play-bills.

Vol. 17, 1849, p. 125

Actors became Mr Punch's target, not so much because of what they said (they were not responsible for the vocabulary in their lines), but because of the way they said it: the contemporary fashion to over-articulate pronunciations—examples are described in *We Are Not Amused*—was a huge source of irritation.

All linguistic ages have their share of uncertain lexical choices. In the Victorian era the relations between the sexes were changing, and as women slowly gained a stronger position in society Mr Punch looked on with some puzzlement.

Clergyman. 'Augustus, wilt thou take this Woman—'
Bride (late of Remnant & Co.'s Ribbon Department). '*Lady!*'

Perhaps a dictionary was the solution? He had been thinking about this from the early days of his magazine.

MATRIMONIAL DICTIONARY

DEAR is a term of entreaty, usually employed before strangers. It is meant to imply affection. It is sometimes used at home, but is generally received with suspicion.

MY DEAR. The above, with a slight infusion of dignity.

DUCK. A term of affection that goes in with the wedding-day, and goes out with the honey-moon.

DUCKEY. The comparative of DUCK.

TOOTSY, MOOTSY, and all words ending in *tsy*, are terms of great endearment. The exact meaning of them has never been ascertained. They are never heard after thirty.

PSHA! A powerful contradiction, or involuntary dissent.

NONSENSE. A negative of intense contempt.

DEARY ME. An exclamation of great impatience—a word expressive of the fidgets.

BOTHER means trouble, irritation, teasing, vexation. It is a word of petulant anger in great request. 'Don't bother me' is equivalent to the French '*tu m'embêtes*'.

LOVE is only used when coaxing is required, as 'Do; there's a love.' It is also a superlative, conveying the highest praise, *ex. gr.*: 'The love of a fellow.' 'The love of a goose.'

TOODLEDUMS. See TOOTSY.

Vol. 11, 1846, p. 135

ex. gr.—exempli gratia 'for the sake of an example'—replaced by *e.g.* today.

He returned to the idea fifty years later, but the tone has changed. There is a gentleness about the early list that is missing here. The impact of the emerging women's movement must have had something to do with it: the National Union of Women's Suffrage Societies would be formed a year later. An article like this next one makes unpalatable reading today, but if we are to represent the vocabulary of the Victorian period fully it should not be ignored.

NEW DICTIONARY
(Being some occasional notes intended as a contribution towards
a 'Lady's Own Dictionary of Words and Phrases.')

'AGGRAVATE.' This word, according to men's dictionaries, means 'to exaggerate: to make enormous, &c.'; but the fair sex, not content with this simple definition, have given it another, which is, to anger, to irritate. For instance, in women's language, the expression, 'an aggravating thing,' is generally understood to signify a person who causes us anger or displeasure. If a man were to talk to a woman of an 'aggravated injury,' she would probably not know what he meant. But if he were to describe her dearest friend's conduct as aggravating, she would immediately understand him.

'SO.' This little adverb is a great favourite with ladies, in conjunction with an adjective. For instance, they are very fond of using such expressions as 'He is so charming!' 'It is so lovely!' &c. According to the rules of strict grammar, the use of the adverb 'so,' and of the adjectives 'lovely' and 'charming,' requires to be followed, in both these sentences, by the use of the conjunction 'that.' 'He is so charming!' is a purely feminine expression. 'He is so charming that I have made a friend of him,' is a purely masculine one, or should be so. It is satisfactory to know, however, that ladies have nothing whatever to do with the rules of strict grammar.

Vol. 110, 1896, p. 11

54

We can sense the early signs of 'political correctness' emerging in a series of long articles headed 'School-Board Papers'. School Boards had been established by the Elementary Education Act of 1870 to provide primary education in places where the existing provision was absent or inadequate, especially for children who came from poor families. During the following decade, the 'three Rs' (reading, writing, arithmetic) were supplemented by classroom subjects such as geography, history and grammar. Mr Punch imagines a situation where a Board has issued formal guidance about the correct use of language, satirizing the upper- (and middle-) class linguistic anxieties in the process. Here are some extracts (there are further examples on pp. 4, 78).

> I say check unruly speech. I may go further, and say never use language that is not largely diluted with water. Never see you loathe a thing, when you have such a harmless word as dislike. Never call people vicious when you can describe them as faulty. Never accuse a man of impudence when you can say he has a little too much confidence; never say he is headstrong when you have such a word as venturesome.
>
> Remember that nothing is atrocious, it is only notorious; that no one is callous, he is only unsusceptible. Remember that no one cheats, he only beguiles; that no one is criminal, he is only illegal; that no one commits a blunder, he is only guilty of an error of judgment.
>
> Things that coarse people would call trash, you must speak of as trifles; things that coarser people would call filthy, you must speak of as dingy; things that both would call gaudy, you must speak of as glittering.
>
> Never forget that people are not fools or foolish, they are simply simple; that they are not vulgarly fat, but pleasantly adipose; that no one gorges, but only fills himself; that murder is softened into despatch; that lies must always be called fibs, and the man who creates lies must be called a fibber. ...
>
> Do all you can to so regulate your speech that no one will notice or care to remember what you say; and, above all, avoid the abusive language which I am sorry to say is creeping even into once respectable journals.

> *Vol. 80, 1881, pp. 12, 14, 33*

THE FRENCH INVASION

If there was one thing Mr Punch hated more than Americanisms, it was pretentiousness, which he located chiefly in the vogue for using French words when, in his opinion, English would do just as well. It is an issue that he returns to throughout the Victorian era, beginning with these articles.

The *negus* was a hot drink of port, sugar, lemon and spice, named after army officer and politician Francis Negus (1670–1732), who is said to have invented it. Gunter is a reference to Gunter's Tea Shop in Berkeley Square, known for its ice creams and sorbets. *Bell's Life*—full title, *Bell's Life in London, and Sporting Chronicle*—was the leading weekly sporting paper of the time, and as English a publication as could be imagined.

NONSENSE THAT IS QUITE REFRESHING

A Morning Paper, speaking of the meeting at the Royal Society, says, 'the refreshments were of the most *recherché* description.' What does this mean? Does it pretend to say that the negus and biscuits were very much run after? or that a person had to look a long time before he could find the cup of tea and muffins which he was dying for? *Recherché* refreshments must be something new. GUNTER probably will be advertising '*Des Glaces très distinguées*,' or pushing his '*Méringues extrèmement comme il faut*.' But we suppose a *recherché* supper means one at which it is the most difficult thing to find anything to eat, after the ladies have retired, and the bread and cheese has to be brought in! The English language is getting so Frenchified, that we expect soon *Bell's Life* will be written in French!

Vol. 16, 1849, p. 176

The allusion in the title Mr Punch gave to this next article is to high-society male fashion—a knot of ribbon or lace worn on the shoulder. Thackeray in *Vanity Fair* (1848, chapter 14) refers to 'The Park Lane shoulder-knot aristocracy'. The 'Hanover Square Temple' is a tongue-in-cheek allusion to St George's church in London's Hanover Square. It opened in 1725, and by Victorian times had become a centre for fashionable weddings. It is regularly described by *Punch* writers as 'the London Temple of Hymen'—alluding to the Greek goddess of marriage. Some years saw over a thousand marriages taking place there, including members of the royal family, statesmen such as Disraeli and Roosevelt, and writers such as Shelley and George Eliot. The church also appeared in fiction. Later, Eliza's father Alfred Doolittle (from Shaw's *Pygmalion*) would be married there.

THE SLANG OF THE SHOULDER-KNOT

Why is a bride called a *fiancée* in fashionable nomenclature; why is a wedding breakfast termed a *déjeuner*; and why are bridal presents said to be of a *recherché* description, instead of being simply described as a choice? Why, when the bride and bridegroom are related to have gone somewhere to spend the honeymoon, are we told that they left town for this place *en route* for that, as if 'on their way' to that would not be sufficiently explicit? Is there anything improper in the English words, and if so, would not Latin be preferable to French?

What is meant by the statement that the service was most impressively read by the REV. MR. SO-AND-SO? Is there any peculiar method on mouthing or spouting the marriage-service wherein the impressiveness of its performance is supposed to consist?

These questions have been suggested by the perusal of the account of a fashionable marriage, celebrated the other day at the old Hanover Square Temple of Hymen. We were in hopes at the footman's French and the other plushisms of high-life reporting had died out: but it appears that these plushy flowers are still flourishing in rank luxuriance.

Vol. 31, 1856, p. 183

In a series of articles on good behaviour, special attention was paid to dining.

In alluding to any article of food, or in drawing up what is vulgarly called a 'bill of fare,' you must always use the French language. You may not understand it, your guests may not understand it, and the servants will certainly not understand it, but for all this it must be used. You must never call soup anything but *potage*, your steak must be christened a *filet*, and the vulgar chop must be softened into the more aristocratic *côtelette*.

The dinner itself is always described as a *dîner à la Russe*. This does not mean that there is one person dining who is very chilly, or is dressed in the Russian costume, nor does it mean that the dishes, or rather fragments of dishes, are served up cold. Any person who thinks that the traditional cold mutton is the real dinner *à la Russe* is thoroughly mistaken. The dinner *à la Russe* is a dinner at which you never see the joints, and are led to believe that you are dining off Christmas-trees, flowers, glass, and Lowther Arcade toys.

Small pieces of food are brought to you from behind a screen, which are called *entrées* not entries. The roast meat is called *rôt*, which is not a vulgar expression, although it looks very much like it, and, being pronounced *roe*, sounds fishy. The fish is always called *poisson*, another curious expression; while beans are called *flageolets*, suggestive of a blow out on musical instruments, and a certain red wine has a name which sounds like French for pomatum. The curiosities of the *menu*, as it is called in place of 'bill of fare,' are so numerous that they are worthy of a separate lecture.

Vol. 80, 1881, p. 14

Punch devoted a long description to this glass-domed shopping arcade in the Strand (*Vol. 4, 1843, p. 235*): it is 'open to the public every day, Sundays excepted, from eight in the morning to an uncertain hour of the evening'. Its 24 small shops at first sold luxury goods, but by the time of this article most had been turned into toyshops. Mr Punch found it a chaotic place:

> The first idea that strikes the visitor upon entering is, most probably, that the houses have been turned out of window; and the contents of their shops shot upon the ground by some architectural avalanche. Indeed, the greatest caution is necessary in threading your way amongst the labyrinth of goods on every side, the most fragile generally being placed where they can be readily kicked over and broken.

LOWTHER ARCADE IN THE 1880s

As the Victorian era approached its close, the menu continued to attract attention—even, at times, reaching poetic heights. The first stanza refers to Maurice Maeterlink (1862-1949), a Belgian writer who received the Nobel Prize in Literature in 1911. At the time of this article he was known chiefly as a playwright. Critics of his writing style would refer dismissively to the way it echoed the repetitive exercises in the 'Ollendorff method' of language teaching—Heinrich Gottfried Ollendorff (1803–1865).

MISCONSTRUCTION

['Some rebellious murmurs have lately been heard against the quaint and pleasing practice of printing the *menu* in French.' *The World.*]

Oh, democratic leveller, who do not even shrink
From turning into English Ollendorffish MAETERLINCK,
Spare yet this further step! nor let your ruthless fingers itch
To tear aside the mask that veils the viands of the rich
The card that hides grim secrets from a too inquiring view
In merciful obscurity—the mispronounced *menu.*

Purées we taste and question not, we count it inexpedient
To set down in plain English each mysterious ingredient;
The rather homely sweet-bread sounds quite dignified, you know,
When served (and priced accordingly) as dainty *ris de veau,*
And he who pays in ignorance of what *hors d'oeuvres* mean,
Might grudge a modest shilling for an oyster or sardine.

Sheer gammon and plain spinach seem more appetizing far
If gallicised to *jambon* and disguised as *épinard*;
Let English beef still decorate its wholesome lean and fat
In semblance of *filet de boeuf*, dressed *à la* this and that,
And honest 'Murphies' swell with pride and satisfaction when
Writ large as *Maître d'Hotel, fondantes*, or *Pomme Parisienne.*

Thus heralded and introduced there's nothing comes amiss,
Hunger has neither eyes nor ears, and ignorance is bliss;
Let us from some unknown *Château* our wry-faced claret sip,
Then pay our monstrous bill, and add the *garçon's* heavy tip,
But—no translation! for in truth no restaurant would dare
Describe its thieving *menu* as an honest Bill of *Fare*.

Vol. 115, 1898, p. 221

One gets the impression, from this next article, that the writers in the *Punch* office were routinely scouring the daily press for their material. The opening reference is to the *Morning Post*, a daily newspaper that paid special attention to events in upper-class society. It was acquired by the *Daily Telegraph* in 1937.

SLANG OF THE SUPERIOR CLASSES

In a list of Fashionable Arrangements for the Week, there was announced the other day by the *Post*,

HON. AUGUSTUS and MISS MACDONALD MORETON's 'danse.'

Here again we have a questionable word between Fashion's favourite inverted commas. In what does a danse differ from a *dance*, except in being spelt wrong, if meant for an English substantive? May the inverted commas be taken to express an editorial disclaimer of responsibility for the peculiar orthography of the word? If the word is to be taken for French, why was the French term used in preference to the English one? Is the Frenchification of the name of the thing signified intended to answer the same purpose as the substitution of Latin in certain cases for the vulgar tongue? Is it designed to disguise the coarseness or indelicacy of the thing? Its effect, on the contrary, is rather to suggest somewhat of that sort; and the '*danse*' of those stylish persons, the HON. AUGUSTUS and his fair relative, seems to bear an analogy to what would be described, in a list of 'Unfashionable Arrangements' which might be published in a journal consecrated to the inferior classes, as a 'hop.'

Vol. 36, 1859, p. 257

THE TECHNOLOGICAL INVASION

The consequence of the Industrial Revolution on English vocabulary was immense. Thousands of new technological terms coincided with a massive increase in scientific nomenclature. Over 150,000 words are in the *Oxford English Dictionary* timeline as having their first recorded usage in the period 1850–1900. This anonymous poet reflects gloomily on how things had gone. The allusion in stanza 5 is to Longfellow's poem 'The Building of the Ship' (1850).

THE NEW POETRY

Away with the older poetical 'plant'
That our ancestors hugged and cherished!
'Tis time that the bygone style of chant
With its perpetrators perished.

Away with the rhymes that represent
Loves, seasons, the Bard's internals
(This last to a much to free extent,
À la Lancet and such-like journals.)

For the times have changed and the Muse's tone,
Since the advent of RUDYARD KIPLING
The ancient restraints are overthrown
That the poet's wit were crippling.

He can now sing in technical terms of things
Like pistons and valves and boilers,
Not Spring, but of locomotive springs,
In the slang of the smoke-grimed toilers.

He can tune his lyre to the *Song o' the Ship*
(Not LONGFELLOW'S *Ship* but a *liner*),
In stokehold and gun-room depict a trip
With the air of a boat-designer.

No matter what handicraft or trade,
The constructor of odes will know it;
In electrical times not born but made
Is the new Polytechnic Poet!

Vol. 116, 1899, p. 185

Most of the new scientific terms had classical Latin or Greek origins. Mr Punch was especially concerned when he noticed their influence on his tailor. The example of the 'Palla Gallica advertisement' is a reference to the military tailors George Paul & Henry Fletcher of New Bond Street, who registered their design for what they called a 'Palla Gallica or long-sided coat' in 1847. The original *palla* was a type of short jacket; *Gallica* 'from Gaul'. The *pallium* was a square or rectangular shawl worn by both men and women in Roman antiquity. Being a neuter noun, the ending should be *tepidum* ('warming')—hence the joke in the final sentence.

THE SCHOOLMASTER VERY MUCH ABROAD

We must deprecate that glut of classical names for common things, which threatens shortly to render Latin and Greek as absolutely necessary for a tailors, hair-dressers, ironmongers, and cook-maids, as it is now for classical tutors at £20 pound a year, and assistants at the British Museum at 4s. 2d. a day.

Soon, if asked 'What's in a name?' any but a polyglot professor must confess his inability to answer. ... Then in garments we have the Greek tongue thus misapplied to the British toggery, a great-coat becoming a *Chlamys*, when the very merit of a great-coat is not to be clammy, or anything of the sort; and the *Palla Gallica* advertisement has been repeated till it has positively palled upon us. But if these dead languages must be galvanized by our tailors, let them at least stick to Grammar, and do not let us be at once puzzled by a 'Pallium,' and provoked by a 'Pallium tepid*us*.' *We* ought not to stand neuter in the presence of such abominably false concord, whatever the adjective may do.

Vol. 15, 1848, p. 187

We are so used to *motor car* and *automobile* today that we need to be reminded it was not at all obvious what to call the new means of transport that arrived in the late Victorian era. As this next article indicates, the frontrunner was *auto-motor*, and there was a great deal of discussion about the family of related terms that would be needed—and, as the cartoon (p. 66) shows, whether there were new inventions around the corner. It contains a great deal of background about the motoring culture of the time.

THE NEW VERB

(As Used in an Automoting Log-book.)

A single word for 'to travel by auto-motor' is apparently required. Like 'to bike,' the verb 'to mote' has been sniffed at by purists. It has, however, been completely conjugated as follows:—

(Very) Active Voice.
Present Tense.
I mote.
Thou stokest.
He looks out for the police.
We run into a lamp-post.
Ye knock a man over.
They pay damages.

Future Tense.
I *will* mote.
Thou shalt come along with me.
He will sit tight.
We shall go twenty miles an hour.
Ye will sell your horses.
They shall eat sausages.

Imperfect Tense.
I was moting.
Thou wast trying to steer.
He was carrying a red flag in front.
We were going four hours a mile.

64

Ye were cussing like anything.
They were giving it up as a bad job.

PERFECT TENSE.
Wanting.

FUTURE PERFECT TENSE.
Wanted.

PLUPERFECT TENSE.
I had walked.
Thou hadst biked.
He had taken a hansom.
We had gone by train.
Ye had 'bussed it.
They had stayed at home.

SUBJUNCTIVE PRESENT.
I *may* mote.
Thou mayest buy me a motor.
He may think better of it. (*Aside.*)
We may start to-morrow.
Ye may meet us.
They may pick up the pieces.

SUBJUNCTIVE IMPERFECT.
I might mote.
Thou mightest mote, if you weren't such a silly guffin.
He might mote, only he can't afford it.
We might mote in the dim future.
Ye might mote, or, on the other hand, ye mightn't.
They might mote, and pigs might fly.

IMPERATIVE.
Mote thou (by moonlight alone).
Let him meet some other gal.
Let us get down, for heavens sake!
Mote ye—or perish in the attempt.
Let them burst.

Participles.
Present: Moting.
Past: Sat upon by coroner.

Passive Voice.
The subject of the above is now passive, and has no further voice
in the matter.

Vol. 111, 1896, p. 213

guffin—This word for a stupid, clumsy person is often used by Mr Punch
(see above, pp. 16, 18, 23). It was popular between the 1860s and 1880s.

HINTS FROM OUR INVENTOR'S NOTE-BOOK
The New 'Motorambulator.'

The turn of the century brought another motoring conundrum. Louise
Michel was a French anarchist (1830–1905). The petrol reference dates
from the 1871 Paris Commune, when women were accused of having used
petrol to set off fires. The image became one of the symbols of the event,
and *la pétroleuse* developed a general meaning of a passionately militant
woman. *Teuf-teufeuse* is a feminine variant of *teuf-teuf*: echoing the sound
of an early motor car, and thus sometimes applied to the vehicle itself.

WANTED—A WORD

[The *Daily Telegraph* of Dec. 6 asks:— 'What is the proper desig-
nation for ladies who work their own motor-cars?' and continues—
'A lady motorist will not do, because we apply it to women who use
these cars as means of conveyance. An engineeriste is cumbersome
and not sufficiently dignified. A motoress might do as feminine for a
mechanic.']

What may we call you, venturous maid,
Who your own motor ply,
And, scorning Man's superfluous aid,
Down Piccadilly fly?

Shall we adopt the slang of France,
And name you *belle chauffeuse*?
Or would you like, by any chance,
The title *teuf-teufeuse*?

Gazeuse of 'siphon' has the force,
And would not suit you well;
Nor *pétroleuse*, for that of course
Suggests LOUISE MICHEL.

And 'scorcheress' with 'sorceress'
Would doubtless be confused;
Motiste looks like *modiste* (of dress)
By Fashion-papers used.

The 'car woman' I thought to pen
With 'charwoman' would rank;
There's only *automotrienne*
Left to fill up the blank!

Vol. 119, 1900, p. 237

Before the arrival of the motor car, it was rail transport, with its many technical terms, that attracted attention. On the whole, the new terminology was accepted without comment, but every now and then something caused ructions, as seen in this letter. I have omitted the various aristocrats who accompanied the royals, all scrupulously listed by Mr. Digney. The mention of 'levelling' in his PS was a reference to the challenge of ensuring that railway lines were laid on an even surface. It was a frequently addressed topic in publications of the time.

LOW RAILWAY LANGUAGE

MR. PUNCH,

These are fast times and I am a slow old gentleman. I have not got reconciled to railways yet; they are too fast for me: too fast, not only in speed, but also in regard to the phraseology which they have introduced into the English language. Here, Sir, is a specimen of disrespectful railway slang, extracted from an account of the return of the Court from Scotland, which appeared in one of our Newspapers whereof the style is usually correct and dignified:—

'On approaching the King's Cross terminus the royal train was shunted into the goods station.'

The ROYAL train was SHUNTED! Allow your mind, Sir, for a moment to dwell on the idea of shunting the QUEEN and the Royal Family. Think of HER MAJESTY and PRINCE ALBERT being *shunted*, and that into the goods station. ...

I do say, and will maintain, that 'shunted' is not a proper expression can be made use of relatively in any way to HER MAJESTY, and I hope it may never again, in that application, offend the eyes of your humble servant,

'POMPONIUS DIGNEY.'

'P.S. Talk of railway levelling! What language can be of more levelling tendency than the railway term 'shunted' in application to illustrious personages?'

Vol. 31, 1856, p. 167

NAMING PLACES

Proper names are, strictly speaking, not a part of vocabulary. There is an old Victorian music-hall joke which went something like this:

FRED—I say, I say, I say, I can speak French.
CHARLIE—I didn't know you could speak French.
Let me hear you speak French.
FRED—Nice, Marseilles, Bordeaux…

This is encyclopedic, not linguistic knowledge: just because one knows a few names in a foreign language doesn't mean one can speak that language. But names should have a place in any cultural overview of vocabulary, for they make up a significant percentage of the words on the printed page, and sometimes they take on a more general meaning that places them firmly within the lexicon, such as our use today of *Whitehall* or *Downing Street* to refer to government. Mr Punch, it seems, was particularly concerned with these more general nuances. In the next article, he questions whether street nomenclature appropriately reflects street architecture.

MODERN STREETOLOGY

Streetology is a modern science, but, like many other of the modern sciences, the more we advance it, the further are we off from understanding it. The present cry is for wide streets, and accordingly wide streets are formed; but, like the gentleman who built a house without a staircase, our architects plan wide streets without any consideration how we are to get into them, or how we are to get out of them. Thus we get plenty of streets, but no thoroughfares; for every new way of any extent or importance is remarkable for its beginning at a place from which no one ever comes, and ending in a quarter to which no one is ever going. We have magnificent preparations made for opening a communication between Cook's Court and Jones's Buildings, but the approach from Cheapside to Blackfriars is still narrow, tortuous, and often inaccessible.

The nomenclature of new streets is conducted on the same absurd principle. The boldest ways have the meanest appellations, while the most illustrious titles are given to the dirtiest lanes and the humblest alleys. We find Smith Streets with foot-pavements twelve feet wide, while Waterloo Street is in some remote hole, through which WELLINGTON could never have brought up a van half the size of one of JULLIEN'S.

Vol. 12, 1847, p. 265

The *Wellington* he refers to is Arthur Wellesley, 1st Duke of Wellington (1769–1852), who defeated Napoleon at the Battle of Waterloo (1815). *Jullien* requires more explanation. Louis-Antoine Jullien (1812–1860) was a French conductor and composer who arrived in London from Paris in 1838 and became well known for his showmanship and flamboyance, and his promenade concerts of light music. 'Monsieur Jullien' became a household name, and *Punch* often caricatures him, from its very first issue. From a linguistic point of view he is famous because he had thirty-six first names (which must be a record). His violinist father wanted a member of his town's orchestra to be the child's godfather, and when every player offered to perform the role, he decided to name the baby after all of them! At the time, a van (a shortened form of *caravan*) was a horse-drawn, usually canvas-covered, vehicle with a square body and flat sides, designed to carry goods. It must have been of some size, to carry the instruments and equipment of his orchestra—hence the allusion to the narrowness of Waterloo Street.

In another attempt to reform street names, Mr Punch looks hopefully at the Metropolis Management Act of 1855, which became law at the end of that year. He makes numerous digs in his selection of new street names, glossed below in parentheses. *Miss Strickland* was Agnes Strickland (1796–1874), known for her twelve-volume *Lives of the Queens of England*, published between 1840 and 1848.

STREET NAMES

Among the numerous benefits which London will derive from the new Act for the Government of the Metropolis, is a revision of the system of street nomenclature. The mass of King Streets, Queen Streets, Victoria Streets, Albert Streets, and the like, will have to sort themselves. To each King Street will be put the Shakespearian question, 'Under which King, Bezonian?' and the Queens will be expected to be equally explicit, and to apply to MISS STRICKLAND for separate christening. Victoria Street (and Punch Street) will be names restricted to the very highest order of thoroughfare, morally, socially, and architecturally considered; and the Albert Streets, with perhaps a couple of exceptions at opposite quarters of the town, will be told off into Consort Street, Hat Street, Night-light Street, and other titles which, preserving affinity, may avoid confusion.

Equal justice will be meted out to the plebeian localities. SMITH and BROWN will not be allowed to stud districts all over with Smith Streets and Brown Terraces, nor will it be held sufficient reason for having eleven Mary-Ann Places in one suburban parish, that eleven respectable and uxorious builders have wives of that name. As for John Street, James Street, William Street, Alexander Street, Henry Street, Edward Street, and all the other streets with mere *praenomina*, they must prepare to take less ridiculous appellations. ...

Some difficulty, it is thought, may arise in the selection of the new titles, and inhabitants who have settled placidly down under the no-meaning names of Pleasant Row, Prospect Terrace, the Paragon, or the simply declarative River Terrace, Thames Bank, or Parliament Street, may rebel against any title which may have more definite associations. But, while respecting this English feeling, let us remind such persons that no vow of allegiance is at present held to be implied by residence in a street with ever so specific a name. Living in Wellington Street does not compel you to go about in Wellington boots, residing in Grosvenor Row does not pledge you to the Sunday Trade Bill, chambers in Regent Street do not make you an admirer of GEORGE TURVEYDROP, a house in Gordon Square does not constitute you a worshipper of LORD ABERDEEN, and you may dwell in Wood Street and yet join the rest of your fellow creatures in considering that the First Lord of the Admiralty no very great statesman. Did a house suit *Mr. Punch*, were there hot and cold water to the top, no black beetles or church bells to be seen or heard, and the taxes reasonable, he would not hesitate to live therein, even though the street were called after MR. DUFFY or MR. CALCRAFT.

The allusions in the last paragraph become increasingly opaque to modern eyes. The Grosvenor reference is to Lord Grosvenor, who in 1855 (the year this article was published) proposed a Sunday trading bill to keep shops shut on Sundays. *George Turveydrop* was presumably Prince Turveydrop, a character in Dickens's *Bleak House*, published in 1853. He was named after George the Prince Regent, and Regent Street was named in the Prince's honour. Lord Aberdeen was the prime minister (1852–55); his name was George Hamilton-Gordon.

The dig at Sir Charles Wood is unclear. He was First Lord of the Admiralty at the time this article was written, but previously a chancellor of the exchequer who was opposed to helping the Irish during the Great Famine a few years before. The Irish question also lies behind the reluctance to name a street after Charles Gavan Duffy, a proponent of Irish independence who emigrated to Australia in 1856, later becoming premier of Victoria. His reputation accompanied him: a cartoon in *Melbourne Punch* (modelled on the English magazine) that year showed him entering parliament as a rustic Irishman carrying a shillelagh. The reluctance to name a street after Mr. William Calcraft needs no explanation: he was the longest-serving hangman in England (1829–74).

Most of the jokes in these next paragraphs will be missed today without a cultural gloss [shown in parentheses]. The 'new Palace of Westminster' refers to the rebuilt Houses of Parliament, following the destruction of the earlier building by fire in 1834. The new Commons chamber had recently been completed (1853).

A Commission, with *Mr. Punch* at its head, will probably issue for the allotment of names, and literature may be enabled to render some assistance in the business. He is not inclined to forestal his work by publishing his whole plan, because in that case Government would probably steal it, and give him no money. But he will furnish a specimen of his notion. He would divide London into districts, and by means of his own immense topographical knowledge—not that he would not be glad of the co-operation of his friends PETER CUNNINGHAM [author of *Hand-book of London, Past and Present*, 1850] and JOHN TIMBS [author *of Curiosities of London*, 1855]—he would decide what feature gave worthiest historical, social, or other characteristic to the prescribed locality. Settling this, the feature in question should give the key to the nomenclature.

Suppose, for instance, that the district included the new Palace of Westminster. This is, evidently, the key required. Parliament Street exists. Add to it Lord Street, Commons Street, Throne Street, Speaker Street, Mace Street, Bauble Street [a reference to the Speaker's Mace], Green-Box Alley [a reference to the despatch boxes carried by permanent secretaries], Black Rod Passage, Lobby Street, Order Street, Bill Street, Vote Street, Count Street, Bore Street, Bribe Street, Profligate and Unexampled Expenditure Street, and so forth. Observe the great advantage of this system. It would make no second title necessary. Who hears the word Bore or Bribe, and does not instantly think of Westminster?

In the final paragraphs on streetology we are treated to a flood of new names that are partly people of contemporary fame and partly in-jokes deriving from the magazine and its launch. Anyone connected with *Punch* would have recognized them immediately. Modern readers are not so lucky (see opposite page). *85 Fleet Street* was, of course, the *Punch* office.

Take another instance. Suppose Drury Lane theatre were the feature of the district whose streets required names. Preserve Drury Lane. And Kemble Street, Kean Street, Young Street, Siddons Street, O'Neill Street, Macready Street, Vestris Street, Braham Street, Malibran Street, Stanfield Street, Grieve Street. Or, if it would not be too humiliating to a respectable locality, even the names of authors and composers, who have in some humble degree contributed to the success of the stars, might be used for the back lanes and by-ways, as Shakespeare Court, Ben Jonson Alley, Beaumont Passage, Fletcher Lane, Sheridan Corner, Rossini Row, Balfe Buildings. One would not be severe, and suggest titles which, though they have no connection with any of the above honourable names, might hit elsewhere, as Rant Street, Stamp Street, Quack Street, Puff Street, Gag Street, Clique Street, and other appellations that might occur to the malicious.

Or, finally, suppose the district to be named included *Mr. Punch*'s Office. How the corner of the streets would sparkle with one constant illumination. Punch Street, Judy Street, Toby Street, would be the grand titles, and despite what has been said about non-allegiance, the rents would go up fearfully from the moment those names went up. Happy too would those lucky householders be whose destiny should plant them in Almanack Street and Pocket-Book Row; happy the dwellers in Caudle Street, Tidmarsh Street, Struggles Street, Pips Street, Briggs Street, Comic England Street, Violet Street, Honeymoon Street, Bib Street, Bashi-Bazouk Street, with those in Wit Street, Humour Street, Wisdom Street, and the other streets which would derive their names from all the Virtues formally resident with BISHOP BERKELEY, but now far more comfortably installed at 85, Fleet Street, London.

Vol. 29, 1855, p. 100

74

GLOSSARY

Almanack Street—the Punch Almanack, an annual issue

Balfe Buildings—Michael Balfe, opera composer (1808–1870)

Beaumont Passage—Francis Beaumont (*c.*1585–1616), playwright

Ben Jonson Alley—playwright (1572–1637)

Bashi-Bazouk Street—Thackeray had made his final contribution to *Punch*
with *Letters from the East by our own Bashi-Bazouk* in 1854

Bib Street—Mrs Bibs, character created by *Punch* writer Douglas Jerrold

Braham Street—John Braham (*c.*1774–1856), opera singer

Briggs Street—a character in cartoons by John Leech, an early contributor

Caudle Street—Mrs Caudle, character created by Douglas Jerrold

Fletcher Lane—John Fletcher (1579–1625), playwright

Grieve Street—Thomas Grieve (1799–1882), theatre designer

Honeymoon Street—recalling the enthusiasm after launching *Punch*

Kean Street—Charles Kean (1811–1868), actor

Kemble Street—surname of an acting family, beginning with Roger Kemble
(1721–1802), and including John Philip Kemble (1757–1823)

Macready Street—William Macready (1793–1873), actor

Malibran Street—Maria Malibran (1808–1836), opera singer

O'Neill Street—Elizabeth O'Neill (1791–1872), actress

Pips Street—Mr. Pips, character created by *Punch* cartoonist Richard Doyle

Pocket-Book Row—the *Punch Pocket-book*, a diary-like publication that
reprinted items from the previous year

Rossini Row—Gioachino Rossini (1792–1868), composer

Shakespeare Court—William Shakespeare (1564–1616), playwright

Sheridan Corner—Richard Brinsley Sheridan (1751–1816), playwright

Siddons Street—Sarah Siddons (1755–1831), actress

Stanfield Street—Clarkson Stanfield (1793–1867), scenery designer

Struggles Street—presumably recalling the difficulties experienced in the
first year of publication

Tidmarsh Street—a Mr Tidmarsh is a character in the first issue

Toby Street—Mr Punch's dog

Vestris Street—Elizabeth Vestris (1797–1856), actress and theatre manager

Young Street—Charles Mayne Young (1777–1856), actor

Violet Street—Miss Violet, created by *Punch* journalist Shirley Brookes

Mr Punch didn't usually have anything to say about the names of towns and cities, but for some reason he became very irritated by what was going on in America.

IMPERFECTION OF THE YANKEE TONGUE

The *New York Times*, whilst glorying in the general inventive powers of Americans, deplores their national deficiency in the faculty of inventing names for places. 'Brownsville,' 'Tomkinsville,' 'McGrawlersville,' are instanced by our New York contemporary as specimens of the inelegant and inexpressive designations which the pioneers of Yankee civilization are in the habit of allotting to newly founded towns and cities, whilst 'Milwaukee' is described as 'a beautiful name.'

There is certainly a difference between 'Milwaukee,' and 'Brownsville,' together with the congeneric 'villes' of TOMKINS and MCGRAWLER, but it is not so much the difference which exists, or may be conceived to exist, aesthetically, between the settlers MCGRAWLER, TOMKINS, and BROWN on the one hand, and the aboriginal BLACK HAWK on the other. The euphony of 'Milwaukee' is very analogous to that of 'Hokey Pokey.' There is a sort of native sweetness in the sound of either name... If the Americans want names of that sort for their new settlements, they might readily obtain them. To a sane adult it might not, perhaps, be a very becoming mental exercise to invent such denominations; but plenty of them might be procured from any nursery, the occupants of which are able to talk; or from any lunatic asylum whose inmates are not deaf and dumb. The invention of funny names like 'Milwaukee,' would be an innocent amusement for infants, and a very suitable employment for the insane, serving in some degree to utilise those unfortunate beings.

Nothing is so easy as gibberish to anybody who will give his mind to it, provided that mind is undeveloped or disordered. It is strange that a people so fertile as our Transatlantic kinsmen in the production of odd words in general should be so slow as they appear to be at local nomenclature. How the nation that has added 'catawampous,' 'slockdologer,' 'stampede,' and 'bogus,' to the English dictionary can be at a loss for terms, racy of the soil, to apply to any portion of it, is difficult to conceive. Can it be a hard matter for those who call each other 'hard-shells,' 'soft-shells,' 'hunkers,' 'locofocos,' 'border-ruffians,' and 'barn-burners,' to call any number of places names? Even if they cannot by natural means accomplish the task of naming new locations, they might avail themselves of the assistance of spirit-rapping mediums, through whom, doubtless, they could get rapped out plenty of words that would answer the purpose at least as well as 'Milwaukee'—words original as to orthography, and of unknown meaning.

Vol. 33, 1857, p. 7

GLOSSARY

barn-burners—nickname for members of the radical faction in the Democratic Party, who wanted to get rid of institutions where there had been abuses, rather than to reform them—the allusion being to the story of the Dutchman who rid himself of rats by burning the barn where they lived.

border-ruffians—name (given by Easterners) for lawless people who lived on the frontier between the occupied and unoccupied parts of the 'Wild West'.

catawampous—fierce, destructive; awry.

hard-shell—a type of turtle having a hard shell > a more conservative member of the Democratic Party in New York state; also a Baptist having conservative views.

hunker—a conservative in politics.

locofoco—a cigar or match > a supporter of a radical faction in the Democratic Party.

sockdologer—a knock-down blow, a finisher. [Mr Punch, or his typesetter, got the spelling wrong in the article.]

soft-shell—a type of turtle having a soft shell > a less conservative member of the Democratic Party in New York state; also, a Baptist having liberal views.

SWEARING

At the end of one of his School-Papers (see above p. 55), Mr Punch recommended his readers to 'avoid the abusive language which I am sorry to say is creeping even into once respectable journals'. That was in 1881. He must have felt despondent, because only twenty-five years earlier he had sensed the opposite trend, as this item illustrates. Some of the clothing terms are unfamiliar today: a *smockfrock* was a loose-fitting garment of coarse cloth, reaching to or below the knee, typically worn by farm labourers; a *highlow* was a short-laced boot reaching to the middle of the lower leg; and an *ankle-jack* was a jackboot reaching above the ankles. The personalities mentioned were all political supporters of the Sunday Trading Bill, which was introduced by Lord Grosvenor in 1855 (see p. 72): Hugh Fortescue, Lord Ebrington (1783–1861) and John Wilson-Patten (1802–1892).

SABBATH-BREAKING AND SWEARING

Swearing is now not only unfashionable, but both unusual and vulgar. An oath is rarely uttered by any individual of the First or Second Class, even when the Collector calls for the Income-Tax. Yet many persons now living can recollect the time, when almost every man, except a clergyman or a dissenter, was accustomed to mingle his discourse with imprecations. At present scarcely anybody whatever in a black coat, or a coat of any other cloth of a woollen texture, and ordinary boots, is in the habit of cursing and using bad language. That habit is nearly confined to the wearers of fustian and velveteen jackets, smockfrocks, nailed highlows, and ankle-jacks. In passing a group of these Third Class people at the corner of a street you too often hear one or more of them pronounce words which cannot be quoted. Now the pronunciation of these words is unnecessary on the speaker's part, offensive as regards yourself, and revolting considered in relation to hearers of a tender age or gentle sex. Nobody doubts the wickedness of this abuse of speech; though a few may possibly question whether the First Day of the week is the Seventh.

If, therefore, LORD ROBERT GROSVENOR, LORD EBRINGTON, MR. WILSON PATTEN, and the other Sabbatarians, persist in pressing or maintaining their Coercion Bills for obliging the common people to observe Sunday by fasting and abstinence, it may be expected that one or more of them will call upon the House of Commons to take some steps to prevent swearing in the streets.

Already there exists a law which renders any person guilty of swearing liable to be apprehended by a policeman, taken before a magistrate, and fined 5s. per profane oath. This law has been lying dormant all that time during which the practice of indulging in execrations has been on the decline.

Will LORD ROBERT GROSVENOR and his holy friends let the decline of bad language go on, or will they create a reaction in favour of blasphemy and foul-speaking by reviving the statute against swearing with additional penalties, and with provisions for being duly enforced?

If they do, of course these polite persons will take care that the act shall apply only to the unfashionable streets and places of public resort, lest the punishment designed to prevent the Whitechapel costermonger from addressing his donkey sinfully, shall alight on the gentleman using a casual expression of a similar quality in Bond Street.

It will then be for the House to consider, whether any person, who can speak good English, habitually employs improper expressions; and whether the swearing which the Saints unite to suppress would not be most effectually put down by the education which the disunited Saints render impossible.

At the same time, perhaps, Parliament will be pleased to inquire, whether the most promising way of getting the people to observe Sunday as the Hebrews observe Saturday, is not to provide them with adequate spiritual instruction—that is to say, with a simple index to those texts which enjoin that observance.

Vol. 29, 1855, p. 11

An alternative to the parliamentary solution was to focus on young children, alerting them to the dangers of swearing.

A PRECAUTIONARY MEASURE

'Now go to School, and be a good Boy. And mind you don't use any rude Words!'

'Rude Words! *Tell* me a few, Mummy, and then I shall *know*, you know!'

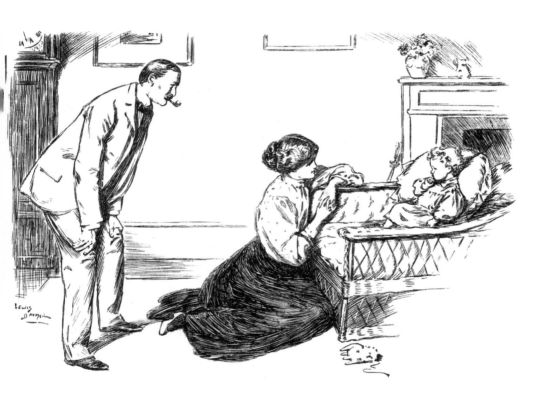

SHOCKING DOMESTIC INCIDENT

Father ⎫
Mother ⎬ *Duet* ⎧ 'Baby say Dad! (*Encouragingly.*)   D—d—d—'
         ⎭   ⎩ 'Baby say Mam! (*Encouragingly.*)   Mam—mam—'
Baby.   'D—d—dam!'

81

Karl Marx, in London when the Sunday Trading Bill was being proposed, was impressed by English swearing. A riot in Hyde Park against the new bill led to this report he wrote for *Neue Oder-Zeitung*, (28 June 1855):

> The spectators consisted of about two-thirds workers and one-third members of the middle class, all with women and children. The procession of elegant ladies and gentlemen in their high coaches-and-four with liveried lackeys in front and behind, did not this time pass by in review—but played the role of involuntary actors who were made to run the gauntlet. A Babel of jeering, taunting, discordant ejaculations, in which no language is as rich as English, soon bore down upon them from both sides. As it was an improvised concert, instruments were lacking. The chorus therefore had only its own organs at its disposal and was compelled to confine itself to vocal music. And what a devils' concert it was: a cacophony of grunting, hissing, whistling, squeaking, snarling, growling, croaking, shrieking, groaning, rattling, howling, gnashing sounds! A music that could drive one mad and move a stone.

First Combatant. '— ! — ! — ! — ! &c.'

Bystander. 'Why don't yer answer 'im back?'

Second Combatant. ''Ow can I? 'E's used all the best Words!'

82

Mr Punch's spirits must have been uplifted by this poetic report. Billings-gate is a district in East London which at the time was famous for its fish market, and also for its profanity. (It was relocated to West India Docks in 1982.) Swearing was often described as 'speaking Billingsgate'. In Thackeray's *Vanity Fair* (1847, chapter 13), Mr. Osborne 'made a few curt remarks respecting the fish, also of a savage and satirical tendency, and cursed Billingsgate with an emphasis quite worthy of the place'. But it seems that times had changed.

'Fader's gettin' better. 'E's beginnin' ter swear again!'

TO A FAIR LINGUIST

['A recent visitor to Billingsgate, who had worked there when a boy, was astonished at the comparative absence of bad language he noticed now.'—*St. James's Gazette.*]

Oh! fisher maiden, who of old
In accents of a vulgar scold
   Vociferated,
Even to you can culture reach
Since now we find your parts of speech
   Are expurgated.

Is it that your once uncouth mind
By modern progress grows refined
   (Or only duller)?
And can you show a soul less black,
To compensate us for your lack
   Of local colour?

Alas! in this degenerate age
Where should we find the average
   If once we struck it?
When Billingsgate's a frost and sham,
While ladies sometimes now say—dash,—
   And bishops 'chuck it.'

Vol. 114, 1898, p. 226

For those who found swearing too much of an effort, technology offered limitless new possibilities.

SCENE—GOLF LINKS

Very mild Gentleman (who has failed to hit the Ball five times in succession). 'Well—'

Up-to-date Caddy (producing Gramophone charged with appropriate Expletives). 'Allow me, Sir!'

[*Mild Gentleman* DOES *allow him, and moreover presents him with a shilling for handling the subject in such a masterly manner.*]

GIVING UP

For some people, evidently, the need to be clear and precise in the use of vocabulary was just too much effort. Very early on, Mr Punch had noticed the problem (see the 1845 cartoon below), but by 1866 he clearly couldn't stand it any more, judging by these two articles, and was especially concerned about its potential effect on the judiciary. Mr. Justice Coleridge was John Coleridge (1820–1894), who became Lord Chief Justice in 1880.

MODERN HIEROGLYPHICS

'I say BILL, 'ave you seen Wotdyecailum?'

'Wot, do you mean Wots'isname?'

'O no, not 'im,—that'ere tother.'

'O, ah! I seed 'im fast enuff.'

VAGUE PEOPLE

MR. PUNCH must have observed a certain class of persons which ought to come under the Vagrant Act, on account of their being wanderers. *Le Juif Errant*, [The Wandering Jew] if he be living now, would be a fool to these wanderers. I am speaking of wanderers in conversation: idle, careless people, too idle to rummage up the right word for the right place, too careless to have any sort of regard for the confusion of their auditors, or the possible results of their own laziness. Their save-ourselves-trouble theory is that one word is as good as another, and their defence is a misapplication of SHAKESPEARE's love-sick observation, viz., that a rose might be called a gasometer, and yet retain its delicious perfume. They have a Vague Dictionary, wherein the words Thingummy, Whatyoumaycallem, Thingummyjig, stand for any substantives, adjectives, or even proper names, and in their Vague Grammar the Personal Pronoun is Whatsisname.

This, the Personal Pronoun of Vagueness, is thus declined:—

	Masc.	*Fem.*	*Neuter.*
Nom. /Acc.	Whatshisname	Whatshername	Whatsitsname
Gen.	Whatshisname's	Whatshername's	———
Dat.	To Whatshisname	To Whatshername	To Thingummy
Voc.	Here, Whatyoumacallem!	———	Hi! Thingummybob!
Abl.	With Whatshisname	With Whatshername	From Thingummy

Dual and Plural.

Nom./Acc.	The Thingummies	The Whatshisnames
Gen.	The Thingummies'	The Whatshisnames'
Dat.	To the Thingummies	To the Whatshisnames

Examples.

Nominative and Accusative. Whatshisname wants Whatsitsname. Whatshername likes Whatshisname when he hasn't got Whatsitsname.

Gen. Dat. Whatshername gave Whatshisname's Whatsitsname to Thingummy. He looked to Thingummy for Whatsitsname.

Voc. Here! Whatyoumaycallem! Is Whatshername going from Thingummy with Whatshisname in the Whatsitsname?

Dual and Plural. Whatshername can't sing to those two Thingummies with Whatsitsname.

> *Q.* Are the Whatsitsnames coming tonight?
> *A.* No, only the Thingummies.

The use of Whatsitsname as a substantive is a little puzzling at first, specially to foreigners. Thus—

> Old Whatshisname sat on a Thingummy the other day.
> Hi! Thingummy, don't you eat my Whatsitsnames!
> There's the Thingummies' Whatsitsname going along there.

Sometimes these pronouns are used in the Vague Grammar for proper names, to save the speaker trouble; thus, for example, as an historical fact:—

> 'Whatshisname first introduced thingummies into whatsitsname.'

which is merely a simple form of —

> 'CADMUS first introduced letters into Greece.'

In quotations the vague pronoun is used *emphasis gratia et causa troublam savendi* [mock Latin: grace and favour emphasis saving trouble]; thus, from Macbeth —

> 'Is this a thingummy I see before me,
> The handle towards my whatsitsname?'

and so on.

This new grammar of Vagueness may possibly come into use in the law courts. It will lessen the Judge's labour, and give rise to endless litigation, which is, to say the least of it, a good thing for the solicitors and barristers, and an encouragement to the framers of our statutes. In the following instance of judgement delivered according to the new rule, we find one instance of Whatyoumaycallem used as a verb.

'It has been well observed by Mr. Justice Coleridge that it was not upon any such refined thingummy as that of Whatshisname that the Thingummies have become in our whatsitsname the last whatyoumaycallem of resorts. In the case of the *Queen* v. *Whatshername*, given at great length in *Whatshisname's Reports*, it was distinctly laid down that a Thingummyjig, unable to come to a unanimous whatyoumaycallem, might be lawfully discharged. But this Court, accepting the sound logical reasoning of Chief Justice Thingumbob, must hold that the whatyoumaycallem of a thingummyjig is no bar to a whatsitsname. The thingummy of the Court below is consequently re-whatyoumaycallem'd.'

Some of the disciples of the New Vague School have adopted certain set phrases for the better conveyance of various meanings, thus, for example, 'All that sort of thing,' 'etcetera,' 'and so forth.'

Instance.— One of the New Vagrants enters a restaurant's, where he is going to dine. 'What'll you take, Sir?' asks the waiter. 'Oh,' says the Vagrant; 'some soup, and—er—all that sort of thing.' By which he means the ordinary three courses. For such vagrants as these the greatest luxury is a café, where they are charged so much for dinner, including wine, and have not to bother themselves with choosing.

The disciples of the new Vague Grammar are those *flâneurs* [idle men about town] whom one meets in the afternoon in Hyde Park, Regent Street, Pall Mall, or Bond Street. Ask them what they are going to do, they don't know. Inquire whither their steps are bent? they cannot tell; saving always that they be not bound for any of the four places above-mentioned, or their Club, when they will be quick enough in giving you the required information.

Vol. 50, 1866, pp. 205, 266

Contemporary readers would have had no difficulty seeing the nature of the vagueness in this next article (dated 23 June 1866), but the modern reader needs some context:

The Quadrilateral—Austria had refused to allow Italy to buy Venetia from them. Italy had allied with Prussia, which declared war on Austria on 16 June 1866, the week before this article appeared. The Quadrilateral was the name given to four Austrian fortresses in northern Italy: Peschiera, Mantua, Verona and Legnano.

The Reform Bill—A Bill to extend franchise to the skilled working class, proposed by the Liberals under Lord Russell, had been defeated a few days before (18 June).

Bulwer Lytton—Edward Bulwer-Lytton (1803–73), known chiefly as a novelist, and one of those fiercely criticised by Thackeray (who had penned many *Punch* articles) for writing stories that glamorized the lives of criminals. Confusing him with Shakespeare could hardly be a greater condemnation of the Vague Person's intellect.

Pounds, shillings, and pence [for younger readers]—One pound consisted of twenty shillings; a shilling consisted of twelve pence; and a penny consisted of four farthings.

VAGUE PEOPLE (AGAIN)

Ask any Professor of the Vague School to give you some information on the present state of European affairs.

Ask him plainly, 'What is the Quadrilateral?'

He will tell you, 'Eh? the Quadrithingummy is a whatyoumaycallem, you know, EUCLID—four sides, well, Austria and Prussia to protect the old thingummy, it's difficult to explain exactly, but *you* know.'

You will then put a leading question, thus: 'It is to protect Venetia isn't it, against the South?'

The Vague Person will give himself no more trouble than is requisite for catching at the suggestion 'Yes, protect Venetia.'

'But what do you mean,' you proceed,' by protecting Venetia against the South?'

He doesn't mean anything, of course, but he says, 'Oh, protecting it against the thingummy in the South; they'd soon pitch into 'em,' he adds knowingly, 'if it wasn't for that.'

Press a Vague Person for some definite information about the Reform Bill and the Re-distribution of Seats. He will explain such subjects lucidly, thus: 'Oh, they want to extend the thingummy, at least, Whatshisname and his party do, and they're going to re-distribute whatyoumaycallems, you know.'

The Vague Person is a superficial reader: he has no capacity for study, nor can he closely apply himself to any one pursuit: he reads the *Times* and several other papers every day, and will tell you that there's 'nothing in 'em.' Remind him of *that* important telegram from Paris, or the dreadful crime which has horrified every one, and he will reply, 'Oh that, yes; ah, I thought you knew *that*.'

The Vague Person makes a great point of keeping his accounts, and then muddles them hopelessly. He is always for dividing by twenty, and reducing everything to shillings. He prefers calculation on his fingers to the shorter methods provided by science. In this sense only can it be affirmed that he has arithmetic at his fingers' ends. In adding up shillings he omits pence up to twopence three farthings; and in reckoning pounds he omits a few shillings here and there, and always sticks to what he calls a round sum, which means to him, any quantity consisting only of two figures, of which one shall be a Nought.

A Vague Person is always busy, and has never any time to spare. He does nothing, and gives himself plenty of time over it. He has an imperfect knowledge of a few quotations from standard poets, which he has acquired less by reading than by hearing. He confuses SHAKESPEARE and BULWER LYTTON, is uncertain about SHERIDAN's lifetime, and is hopelessly at fault as to WYCHERLEY, CONGREVE, CHAUCER, 'and that lot,' as he expresses it....

There are many wonderful creations in the world, whose present or ultimate use is a mystery to our limited intelligences. And these Vague People, to what end do they exist? Heaven only knows: apparently, they are useless; certainly they are, save as regards themselves, harmless.

THE PERILS OF COLLOQUIAL PHRASEOLOGY

Kindly Person. 'Care to have a squint at the paper, Sir?'

Lady. 'And what sort of person is Mrs Robinson, Colonel?'

Colonel. 'Oh, the sort of person who calls a table-napkin a serviette.'

Lady. 'But I always call it a serviette.'

Colonel (undefeated). 'Then you know exactly what sort of a person she is.'

ANOTHER FLOWER OF AMERICAN SPEECH

Fair New Yorker (to over-fêted Englishman). 'Say, you're rather a dim bulb
to-night, aren't you?'

THE MORE THINGS CHANGE...

As the Victorian era is left behind, new slang replaces old, new fashionable expressions come and go, and old antagonisms resurface. The trends noted above continued into the twentieth century, as these last few cartoons from the 1920s illustrate. If Mr Punch were still around today—I still deeply regret his forced retirement in 2002—he would have no shortage of examples of twenty-first-century usage to pillory. But, amusement aside, he would be wasting his time. If there is one lesson to be learned, by looking back at the preceding pages, it is the inevitability of language change, and the way one century's anxieties are the next century's acceptances. Who today would get upset at such words as *reliable* and *recuperate*, which aroused such emotion in the 1860s? The new words that were found to be useful have been steadily assimilated; those that were not have silently disappeared. And the language carries on growing, as it always has.

"URBI ET ORBI."

Mr. Punch returns his best thanks to all and singular, the Public and the Press, for the enthusiastic reception with which the toast of his Jubilee, everywhere and by everybody, has been received. To Everyone Health and Happiness, Peace and Prosperity.

Punch.

FURTHER READING

Altick, Richard D. 1996. *'Punch': The Lively Youth of a British Institution, 1841–51*. Columbus: Ohio State University Press.

Crystal, D. 2004. *The Stories of English*. London: Penguin.

—— 2011. *The Story of English in 100 Words*. London: Profile.

—— 2017. *We Are Not Amused*. Oxford: Bodleian Library Publishing.

—— and B. Crystal, 2002. *Shakespeare's Words: A Glossary and Language Companion*. London: Penguin. Online at www.shakespeareswords.com.

Hughes, G. 1988. *Words in Time: A Social History of the English Vocabulary*. Oxford: Blackwell.

Hughes, G. 2000. *A History of English Words*. Oxford: Blackwell.

Phillips, K.C. 1984. *Language and Class in Victorian England*. Oxford: Blackwell.

PICTURE CREDITS

WORD INDEX

aggravate 54
ally 32
ankle-jack 78
A1 4
atrocious 55
auto-motor 64
automotrienne 67
awful 28
awfully 21

barn-burner 77
baw 9–10
beaver 9–10
beery 19
bender 9–10
benjamins 24, 26
Billingsgate 83–4
bill of fare 58, 61
bloke 23
blub 12
blunder 55
bob 9–10, 24, 26
bogus 76
bollinger 9–10
bolt 11
border-ruffian 77
bother 53
brick 9–10, 18, 20–21, 23
bricksy-wicksy 18
broady 24, 26
broom 30
brusquerie 14

buffoned 20
burgle 37
bus 30

cad 12
callous 55
car 47
cartoon ix
catawampous 76
catechism 21
caudle 10–11, 75
chap 23
Château 61
chauffeuse 67
cheap swell 22
cheddar 9–10
cheese 9–11
chlamys 63
chum 10
claim 40–41
claret-jug 11
cleaned out 19
cockywax 22–3
concern 9–10
cool 11
côtelette 58
couter 24, 26
cove 23, 25
crib 9–10, 24, 26
criminal 55
cut, go on the 9, 11
cut, the 9–10

GENERAL INDEX

Aberdeen, Lord 72

actors 51

Addison, Joseph 6

Alabama affair 36–7

Albert, Prince 17–18

Alford, Henry 44

Altick, Richard D. 27

Americanisms vii, 4, 24, 33–47, 76–7

Austen, Jane 44

Balfe, Michael 75

Beaumont, Francis 75

Bedford, Paul 17–18

Bell's Life 56

Billingsgate 83–4

Braham, John 75

Bright, John 6, 45

Brookes, Shirley 75

Brougham, Henry 20

Buckstone, John Baldwin 42

Buckle, Thomas Henry 6

Buffon, Comte de 20

Bulwer-Lytton, Edward 90–91

Burke, Edmund 6

business slang 24–7

Calcraft, William 72

Campbell, Lord 30

Charivari, Le viii

Clarke, Marcus 2

classical loanwords 63

Coal Hole 30–31

Cockney 27

Coleridge, John 86, 89

Cremorne 17, 19

Crichton, Admirable 20

Cruikshank, George 17

Cunningham, Peter 73

Dickens, Charles 4, 16, 20, 27, 34, 72

dining 58, 60

Disraeli, Benjamin 57

Doyle, Richard 75

Duffy, Charles Gavan 72

Ebrington, Lord 78–9

Eliot, George 14, 57

episcopal English 50

Etna, S.S. 42

fast men 16–17

Field Lane 16, 18

Fletcher, Henry 63

Fletcher, John 75

Four in Hand club 22

French words 56–61

functional shift 43

George IV 17–18

Gibbon, Edward 6

Gladstone, William 6, 45

Grant, General Ulysses S. 42